REDEEMING THE WOUNDED:

A PRISON CHAPLAIN'S JOURNEY INTO CRIME VICTIMS ADVOCACY

B. Bruce Cook

Copyright © 2010 by B. Bruce Cook

Redeeming The Wounded:
A Prison Chaplain's Journey Into Crime Victims Advocacy
by B. Bruce Cook

Printed in the United States of America

ISBN 9781609572990

All rights reserved solely by the author. The author guarantees all contents are original and do not infringe upon the legal rights of any other person or work. No part of this book may be reproduced in any form without the permission of the author. The views expressed in this book are not necessarily those of the publisher.

Unless otherwise indicated, Bible quotations are taken from The Eugene Peterson's *The Message*. Copyright © 2002 by NavPress Publishing. Used by permission.

www.xulonpress.com

ABOUT THE AUTHOR

Crime Victims Advocacy Council
3101 Paces Mill Road NW
Atlanta, Georgia 30339
770-333-9254
www.cvaconline.org

Rev. Dr. B. Bruce Cook served as Chaplain and Director of Pastoral Care for the Crime Victims Advocacy Council (CVAC) from 1999 to 2009 in Atlanta GA. He was also commissioned as a 10-10-10 Missionary by the General Board of Global Ministries from June 2002 to June 2005 to serve crime victims in Atlanta. An endorsed Chaplain since 1990 through the Section on Chaplains and Related Ministries (now known as UMEA) of the General Board of Higher Education and Ministry, he was given a GBGM grant to recruit, train and supervise crime victims chaplains across the country from November 2005 to November 2006. He is an affiliate member of AAMFT, NOVA, ACA, and is trained by ICISF, UMCOR and the Red Cross as a disaster chaplain.

Chaplain Cook founded CVAC in 1989 after his step-brother was murdered in 1977. He was ordained in 1971 and appointed to three different chaplain positions by the North Arkansas Conference to serve a county jail, federal prison and crime victims. He served and ministered to victims of serious violent crime in 19 counties surrounding Atlanta, which is in the North Georgia area. His reason and rationale for accepting this call to missionary service lies in Jesus' word in the Good Samaritan Parable to help the wounded crime victim by providing unlimited mercy and compassion.

Chaplain Cook believes the church can provide spiritual healing to those suffering from violent crime. He offers pastoral care in individual, group, family, and support group sessions and guides crime victims through the maze of court hearings, filing for victim compensation, restitution, victim impact statements, and victim notification. He offers prayer and coping skills to those suffering from trauma after the crime (PTSD, Acute Stress Disorder, inability to relax, sleep or work normally). He operates a 24-hour crisis hotline in which crime victims call him for help and referrals. He conducts an annual memorial service for families who had a murder, which is a healing service at the beginning of National Crime Victims Rights Week in April. He has more than 3,500 names on memorial walls who have been murdered in Atlanta since 1991. Crime prevention/victim education safety tips are available by request.

Chaplain Cook believes in the connectional structure, and UM churches partner with him in prayer and with financial and volunteer support to help crime victims. As Christians we are all called to obey Jesus' words in the Good Samaritan Parable to "Go and do thou likewise." Any church in the USA who cares for the wounded victimized neighbor can be in a covenant relationship with CVAC and Chaplain Cook will offer to help any church start a support group for crime victims or conduct a memorial service. After September 11 the nation needs spiritual care and healing for the horrible bombing of the World Trade Center, Pentagon and crashed airplane in Pennsylvania. Chaplain Cook spent a week counseling victims of crime of the WTC in NYC.

He held four jobs with agencies that are part of the U.S. Department of Justice for almost 25 years, LEAA, OAI, U.S. Parole Commission, and Bureau of Prisons. He retired as a federal prison chaplain in 1999 and retired again as a crime victim's chaplain in 2009. His wife, Claudia, is a retired elementary school teacher. Chaplain Cook received his B.A. in religion from Rhodes College and his M. Div. and D. Min. from Drew Theological School. He attended Princeton Theological School. He has a Master's in Public Administration from Georgia State University.

Chaplain Cook received two national awards: one from the Foundation for Improvement of Justice and another from the Office of Victims of Crime signed by President Clinton. The Foundation award was especially nice. They gave him a $10,000 check, which he donated to CVAC. His passion is for making disciples of Jesus Christ and alleviating suffering of crime victims in the Lord's name. His pastoral counseling strengthens churches and congregations by working with and helping local clergy and laity and family members of crime victims respond effectively when there is a murder or violent crime among the "churched or un-churched." He would love to see CVAC chapters and chaplains for crime victims across the USA and see crime victim ministries in every area in support of God's business—the ministry of reconciliation and restorative justice.

Epilogue

*A*s victims of crime we can speak the truth to each other within the context of a support group, and engage in the healing process. We first have to admit that the crime hurt us deeply and we do not know how to cope with it.

We see answers, but we are usually living out and clarifying the right questions. We need somewhere safe and confidential where we can tell our stories to each other about the crime that brought us to the point of needing help in a support group. We need others to listen deeply and to care about us and our pain and grief. We need to feel, believe and sense the struggle of the entire group in order to work on making us better instead of bitter. Each member of the group is equal in the ability to share and respect one another's comments. Each member can help each other clarify his or her true feelings even when the one speaking cannot see the deeper feelings. The healing is always a work in progress but one worth taking.

Don't steal.

Don't lie.

Don't deceive anyone.

Don't swear falsely using my name, violating the name of your God. I am God.

Don't exploit your friend or rob him.

Don't pervert justice. Don't show favoritism to either the poor or the great. Judge on the basis of what is right.

Don't spread gossip and rumors.

Don't just stand by when your neighbor's life is in danger. I am God.

Don't secretly hate your neighbor. If you have something against him, get it out into the open: otherwise, you are an accomplice in his guilt.

Don't seek revenge or carry a grudge against any of your people.

Love your neighbor as yourself. I am God.

Keep my decrees.

Leviticus 19:11-13; 15-19. The Message by Eugene Peterson

Preface

What does it mean to be a Christian chaplain today and minister to those in prison or victimized by crime? What does one do, and what experiences occur with the job? Are there any advanced indicators of what the job may entail? What kind of vision emanates from the experiences of being a chaplain? Why and how would one choose to be a jail chaplain, prison chaplain or chaplain for crime victims as opposed to becoming a traditional pastor, a hospital or military chaplain or a pastoral counselor? What is the difference?

This book addresses these questions and many more. As a retired chaplain, I can say with the test of experience that it is important to try to do what the Holy Bible says. I have listed Scriptures that are basic to the chaplaincy at hand. I have succeeded at times and I have failed at times. I have learned a few things in more than 39 years that I hope will benefit my readers so they will not make the same mistakes I did. I have in my mind a vision that the criminal justice system should exist first for the sake of the crime victims, second for the public or community that was harmed, and last for the offender. Our first duty as Christians is to take the victimized to the Inn of healing and pay whatever it costs and do whatever it takes for the victim to get well after a crime (Luke 10:25-37).

There are many rooms in that Inn of healing, and some can be operated by police, courts, corrections, victim advocates, prosecutors, police chaplains, crime victims' chaplain, hospital chaplains, corrections staff, prison chaplains and clergy and lay leaders of all faiths. For the Inn of healing crime victims to work our entire society would have to dramatically change. Society would need to orient itself toward the healing of crime victims first.

The vision of that Inn of healing coming from the churches, the temples, the tribes, the synagogues and the mosques and supported by the actions of the criminal justice system is real. It just takes some hard work and focus. Let us bring it into being together.

I want to thank my wife, Claudia Cook, my editor Sarah Anne Shope, my friends and colleagues, and all the prisoners and crime victims that helped shape this book. Names and events have been altered to protect the persons from harm and violations of their privacy. Actual names of crime survivors were used by permission.

Thanks to all the crime survivors who blessed me with their truth, honesty, resilience and courage. I use the common words, crime victims, but I always mean crime survivors. May God bless all our chaplains wherever they serve!

B. Bruce Cook
Atlanta, Georgia

Table of Contents

Introduction xv
Chapter 1: Jail Chap 21
             Some Statistics from the Bureau of Justice Statistics:
             An Overview of the Jail and Prison Problem in the
             USA 42
             Facts about the Morris County Jail and the
             Thresholds Program 46
Chapter 2: The Federal Prison Chap 50
Chapter 3: Crime Victims Chaplain 89
Chapter 4: Forgiveness...97
Chapter 5: Overview of Crime 114
Chapter 6: The Three R's: Reconciliation, Redemption and
             Restoration 119
Chapter 7: The Need for Support Groups for Victims of Crime ... 128
Chapter 8: Survivor Stories..135
             Holly Phillips..135
             Julie Allen...139
             Joanne Thomas..141
             Gail Laney 146
             April Shaw...148
             Rhonda Kastl/Kellie Wiggins..151
             Norma Jean Hassell 158
             Claudia Barnes 162
             Angela Sears...165
Chapter 9: The Role of Chaplain 175
Conclusion: A Call to Action 181

Recommendations from the Field for Restitution........................189
References..197
Appendices
        A: Resources 201
        B: Restorative Justice: An Annotated Bibliography...204
        C: Message on New Direction 214
        D: Recommendations from the Field for the Faith
            Community 216
        E. Sample Victim Impact Statement.........................228

INTRODUCTION

Start with a wrong assumption, it will lead to a wrong outcome. If you want to correct a person for wrongdoing, you cannot do so by secretly desiring only to punish that person.

The corrections system does not correct people nor does it make things right after a crime. The system does a good job of isolating the criminal for the purpose of public safety, but all too often at the same time it insures the criminal's return. If two thirds return every few years, the system is perpetuated yet it does not solve the problem of crime.

The reason the criminal justice system does not make things right is because ninety percent of the time it is focused on the criminal instead of on the victim of the crime. A system based on equity and parallel justice for offender and victim would focus on each fifty percent of the time. That kind of 50-50 equity would cause a rebalancing of the entire system of justice in this country. I think it's time has come.

The reason the assumptions about the system are wrong is that it was called a *criminal justice system* in the first place. The resources to apprehend, prosecute and incarcerate the criminal are paramount and well vested. As my good friend, James A. Rowland, former Commissioner of the California Department of Corrections, used to say, "We should have called it the *victim justice system* and then the focus would be on the one harmed."

How do we as a nation bring about a change of thinking in order to make the system equitable after a hundred years of having built up the correctional industrial complex and the power of the state to prosecute? One of the hurdles is that the system is internally and externally flawed. The internal flaws arise from its imbalance towards the offender's rights and needs at the expense of those of the victim's. The system is externally flawed due to the police and courts having a goal to increase recidivism (make arrests and get convictions to keep the public safe), and corrections having a conflicting goal to decrease recidivism (change criminal behavior into law-abiding behavior). Corrections will never succeed if police are aggressively doing their job to apprehend and arrest criminals (and they *should* be aggressive, I might add). Corrections will never succeed if the public wants to pay 95% of the corrections' budget for retribution and punishment and then throw in only a 5% for rehabilitation.

So, if we get off the goal of punishment, what is left—deterrence, public safety, rehabilitation, prevention? Why not consider two new goals for the criminal justice system: crime reparation and a *real* attempt at rehabilitation?

I use the term *rehabilitation* carefully because it is hardly definable today. No one knows what habilitation is or looks like, so how can anyone be rehabilitated? Criminals who are released and commit crimes but are not caught—are they rehabilitated or just smarter criminals? Criminals who reduce the seriousness of repeat crimes—are they rehabilitated or just a less serious crime committer? An alcoholic thrown in the drunk-tank only two times instead of two times in a year—is he rehabilitated by being marginally improved?

Another reason it is difficult to know if a person is rehabilitated is that we do not dedicate or even have the resources to pay for qualitative and quantitative research related to whether or not a person actually is rehabilitated. This is because we do not pay for control group studies to measure positive outcomes or recidivism. I use the term *recidivism* carefully because it is indefinable in many ways. In fact, we have trouble clearly defining it at all. Is it re-arrest within one year, two years, or three years? Is it reconviction within one year, two years, or three years? Is it re-confinement within one year, two years or three years? Is it reduction of the seriousness of repeat crime within one, two, three years? I have just given 12 definitions of recidivism based on years and categories. The definitions increase as we distinguish between re-arrest, reconviction, and return to prison for all crimes, felonies only and misdemeanors only.

There are research statisticians who could conduct studies by running all the statistics against all the definitions of recidivism until they find the most positive outcome and then report that one. According to the National Advisory Commission on Standards and Goals, the definition of recidivism is reconviction within three years of release. While it helps to have one standard definition, I would not want to only measure recidivism as the sole criterion for success of a correctional program and I don't think the public would either. I want to know if the released criminal gets and keeps a job, obtains a GED or educational degree, and based on urinalysis there is evidence that he stops using drugs. I want to know if he stops being a criminal or doing crime. In short, I want him to stop harming people.

Usually the corrections industry reports anecdotal evidence as success of a correctional program. For example, I once heard a jail volunteer program director say his program was 100% successful because he never saw any of the program graduates back in his jail. I asked him how long he had been director and he said, "two years." He had twenty graduates and he never asked for a criminal record check to see if they had been rearrested in another county, rearrested on a new state or federal offense, or if they had gone to state or federal prison. He just knew they had not returned to his jail based on his observation. He also had no comparison or control group to measure his successful graduates against. He could have picked a random twenty out of the jail, given them no program at all, and he might say he never saw them back in his jail either.

If there is a rigorous research design to randomly assign persons into the treated and non-treated groups and if the program researchers measure several outcomes, such as recidivism, job retention, drug usage, and so forth, then the study has to go on for several years. The corrections system rarely pays for such longitudinal studies. That is what led Robert Martinson to say in the 70s that in the field of corrections that "Nothing works." I think what he really meant to say was that due to the scarcity of even rudimentary carefully controlled research he could not find many studies that proved or disproved that a particular program worked with the prisoners who experienced it. The research designs were so often flawed that no conclusions could be drawn.

As my good friend, Ellis MacDougal, a corrections commissioner in several states used to say "Rehabilitation does not work because we have never really truly tried it." Sadly, he is right even today because we as a society do not know what rehabilitation looks like for a released prisoner and we do not adequately pay for it and then measure it with good quality research. As a result, crime continues at an alarming pace and many good people suffer at the hands of criminals.

Crime reparation is not new, but it would be ground-breaking if it were emphasized as the primary goal of the criminal justice system. Police would behave differently and would insure crime rights were as important as criminals' rights, such as with Miranda and disclosure rights. Police would really work towards returning property to victims and keeping them safe from retaliation by the criminal. Police, advocates and chaplains would be at the scene of a lot more crimes to offer counseling to the victims.

To be reparative, prosecutors would have to give up a lot of their power to let crime victims and their supporters and offenders and their supporters work on family group conferences, circle sentencing and restorative justice practices when the crime involves theft and fraud and especially with juvenile offenses that were not violent. To be reparative, corrections would need to involve a lot more restitution and community service from ex-inmates, probationers and parolees. There would be victim impact panels and victimology courses required of every inmate using video and manuals of instruction. Chaplains, counselors, case managers, psychologists, volunteers and educational staff would all be trained to emphasize to the inmate that he should make amends for the crime by accepting responsibility, apologizing, and participating in inmate financial responsibility to pay restitution, fines, family support and to a victims fund. The correctional system should exist primarily to make things right as nearly as possible for the victim.

I hope these comments intrigue you a bit and you want to know more. This book is about some reflections from a jail chaplain, a federal penitentiary staff chaplain and a chaplain for crime victims. Some of these experiences might shed some light on the need to change our current criminal justice system into a victim-centric justice system.

What God reveals in the Holy Bible:

(Scripture taken from THE MESSAGE Copyright 2002. Used by permission of NavPres Publishing Group. All rights reserved.)

"So, chosen by God for this new life of love, dress in the wardrobe God picked out for you: compassion, kindness, humility, quiet strength, discipline. Be even tempered, content with second place, quick to forgive an offense. Forgive as quickly and completely as the Master forgave you. And regardless of what else you put on wear love. It's your basic, all-purpose garment. Never be without it.

Let the peace of Christ keep you in tune with each other, in step with one another. None of this going off and doing your own thing. And, cultivate thankfulness. Let the Word of Christ—The Message—have the run of the house. Give it plenty of room in your lives. Instruct and direct one another using good common sense. And, sing, sing your hearts out to God! Let every detail in your lives—words, actions, whatever—be done in the name of the Master, Jesus, thanking God the Father every step of the way." Colossians 3:12-17. *The Message* by Eugene Peterson

CHAPTER 1

THE JAIL CHAP

Photo by Mike DuBose, United Methodist News Service

**It is a tremendous inequity to minister to prisoners
and their families and not to victims and their families.
Rev. Bruce Cook**

I guess it was in my DNA to be a minister, but if you'd known me in my early years of throwing mud pies at the neighbor's homes and behaving as a spoiled brat at times, you would never have guessed it. I was a typical self-absorbed, rudderless teenager when God, or fate, or Life got my attention. I was in a serious car wreck at 15 and wondered if I would live. While lying on the grass with my teeth knocked out, my face all bloodied and my leg and ankle torn, I said feebly "I don't know if you are really there, but if you are, Jesus, and you get me through this, I will promise my life to you." Just then warm light came over me and I felt peace and calm. I started as a baby Christian on that day and soon began going to Sunday school, Young Life, and Fellowship of Christian Athletes. I really changed. Now I had a rudder and knew where I was headed—in the direction of Jesus.

My father was the son of a Baptist minister, and he attended Sunday school and church regularly, so I went with him. But not until the car wreck did God have my heart. When I first got a license to preach at 18, I was nervous about preaching to the same people I had thrown mud pies at. I was so nervous I forgot my entire memorized sermon on a Sunday evening service. The minister called me up to the pulpit and grabbed my hand and said calmly, "This is this boy's first sermon and I want him to know if he just says two words, Jesus Christ, his whole sermon will be victorious." He looked at me with gray hair and blue eyes softened by years of Christian faith that galvanized and anointed me with the Spirit. I preached to everyone in that Spirit, pounded the pulpit, and changed my sermon to address some of their needs. In that moment I truly was blessed and guided by the Spirit of the Risen Christ. I was His cheerleader and I was bringing to them His message of hope, of love and forgiveness.

Dad tells a story of his father who preached in Horse Cave, Kentucky. A farmer used to bring two chickens and put them under the pew. After the sermon he would shake my grandfather's hand and hand him the chickens as his tithe. One time he did not like one of the sermons. He shook hands, tore off a wing and silently gave the wing to my grandfather. He took the rest of the chickens home. After my first sermon, my dad came up afterwards and said, "Son that was a two-chicken sermon."

No one fifth-grader ever says when asked what you want to be when you grow up that "I want to be a prison chaplain or a chaplain for crime victims." In fact, I thought for years that I wanted to be a Professor of Religion in college, like my professors at Rhodes College, until I got to seminary and said, "I cannot study this material forever—it is theory without action and will kill my spirit." Then I did not know what to do or what I wanted to do, or better yet what God wanted me to do.

After a year and a half as a YMCA Youth Director, I stumbled on the job placement board in Drew Theological Seminary that the

Morris County Chaplaincy Council was looking for a Morris County Jail Chaplain in Morristown, New Jersey. I interviewed and got the job.

The first thing I noticed in 1970 was that there was no on-the-job training or training materials available for this position. I was actually thrust into it without any warning or training. I was appointed by the Bishop in Arkansas to the jail extension ministry, but I was not yet endorsed by the ecclesiastical body, called the Section on Chaplains and Related Ministries in Nashville, Tennessee. This eventually became the United Methodist Endorsing Agency. Later on I did receive this denominational endorsement, which is important to the extension ministry, and in fact, some agencies like the federal Bureau of Prisons will not hire you as a chaplain without it.

One of the first things I had to do as a jail chaplain was to find space for an office so I could do some work. Previous chaplains had worked from their home. I asked the Morristown YMCA if they would let me have a classroom space without charge and they agreed. It was a block from the jail, which made it very convenient. My former YMCA experience helped me.

The first time I walked into the Morris County Jail I noticed the smell. The doors clanked shut and I was in a jail. I was locked up. Little did I know that almost every jail, state or federal prison, or correctional institution of any kind, has its own smell—something like cleaning fluid mixed with sweat and dirty socks. It was mixed with the odor of inmates who didn't care too much about washing up very often.

I felt confined, a bit claustrophobic and somewhat scared. One of the officers told me something I never forgot. He said, "Chap, don't ever let 'em see any fear in your eyes or they know they have you and they can play you. Never, ever show fear." That helped a lot, and I decided to calm my fears and hide them. The first time I gave a sermon in that jail, my stomach felt like I had eaten a garlic pizza and followed it with rubbing alcohol.

This was a little county jail in New Jersey with a capacity of a little over a hundred inmates. Most of the sentenced inmates did an average of about 45 days. They had to be sentenced to less than a year to be there, and if sentenced to over a year, they went to state prison. Some were awaiting trial, and that could range from any crime of tax evasion to murder. The Annual Report of the Jail in 1972 revealed that the inmates were mainly young with a mean age of 25 — 82.5% white, 53% single, and 94% male. Their crimes were for theft 24%, drugs 23%, violent crime 11%, probation violation 11%, failure to appear in court 10%, motor vehicle violation 8%, disorderly conduct 8%, and miscellaneous conduct 5%. They were poorly educated to the junior high level, semi-skilled workers, with a lot of drug and alcohol abuse. There was a high rate of turnover and in 1972, when only 23% were in the jail for longer than 30 days. As I looked at these guys with missing teeth and tattoos and muscle shirts, I could not help but wonder, "What the heck have I gotten myself into here?"

In seminary we talked a great deal about answering the call that God has given to you. I had just taken a job that was on a board so I could pay for seminary, but it was God calling, which I soon figured out. Why? It was low pay in a jail that smelled and was cut off from society. There was absolutely no status to the job. It was very hard work walking the tiers daily, listening to inmate's concerns, visiting the sick inmates, counseling them and their families, and giving sermons every week for three years with no backup. No one in his right mind would want such a job.

On the other hand, it was a street kind of ministry and I always found Jesus in the street alongside me. The Kinney program at Rhodes College taught me that ministry to people was out in the community, and if you think about it, Jesus spent most of his time walking and talking in the community. He spent very little time preaching in the synagogues.

The main reason I knew it was God calling was because it was pure joy to work with the inmates and their families, the staff and the volunteers. As I have often heard, joy is when you place Jesus first, Others second and You last, spelling J-O-Y. The command of Jesus in Matthew 25 is to minister "to the least of these" who are sick or in prison. That command got me here, even if it is roundabout.

I also had this awareness that maybe Jesus and Paul were the first prison chaplains when they were confined in Roman jails. Paul wrote material from jail and so did Martin Luther King in his Letters from Birmingham Jail. Dietrich Bonhoeffer wrote letters from prison. God was just as present in prison as out of prison. I did not need to bring Him there as He was already there. I just needed to connect Him.

The Call was a warm call then because I could feel and sense that God was in the call. A warm call occurs when God wants you to do something and you feel good about it in your heart and it seems to be what you wanted to do with your life. The warm call is a perfect fit. A cold call occurs when God wants you to do something and you don't want to do it. It seems like a duty or obligation, like something you should do for God but definitely not one you feel good about doing or even want to do. It is uncomfortable and does not fit your plans. Kind of like Noah must have felt building an ark in the middle of a desert. Some of working in jail as a chaplain felt a little like a cold call.

I have no doubt that God wanted me to visit the persons in that jail and give them the gospel of Jesus Christ. He wanted me to be a Jesus-like person to them, which by any other name is being a chaplain. Care and comfort. Listen and counsel. Teach and exhort. Pray for healing. Pray for new life and new direction for each inmate. Minister to inmates, staff and volunteers. That was my training and that was my calling. It was a path that had a heart in it, as my grandmother used to say.

Being a chaplain is a noble profession. I hardly ever hear of a scandal involving a chaplain in the military, hospital, pastoral counseling, prison, jail, hospice, crime victims, life coach, or mental health chaplain. Occasionally, they get fired for being naive or giving away the store to inmates, but rarely do I hear of a scandal of a chaplain in a public forum. There are exceptions. Chaplains are human and sometimes make mistakes, which I will go into later.

Over the years the profession of chaplaincy has become organized and credentialed, but back when I started out, the credential was that I was a warm body. I was just as naïve as anyone else. I got lied to about 5000 times in those three years by different inmates in that small county jail. I was told the truth about 250 to 500 times, figuring about 5 to 10 percent of the time I got the truth. As my experience with inmates grew, I learned to tell the difference when one was lying and when one was telling the truth. Truth was running closer to five percent of the time then. It was good training even if it were by trial and error.

I remember the day-shift sergeant telling me, "Chap, there are three kinds of inmates in this jail: C, C and C, which stands for Cream Puffs, Career Criminals and Coconuts. The Situational guys, or Cream Puffs, are here one time, and jail gets to them and they do not want to come back and they don't, so there is no need focusing too much time on them. Career Criminals cannot be changed, and they are here over and over. Jesus Christ could walk in here and not change them a bit. So, dust them off your shoes and walk on. Next are the Coconuts—they could fall either way—either a Situational Criminal or a Career Criminal. Those Coconuts you need to spend time with because they might be open to change and some suggestions. You might change one of them from being a burglar or a robber to a paper hanger or check forger, or to doing no crime at all. Learn to be happy with small changes, too."

When I asked how he knew which were which, he said, "In five minutes of talking to them you can figure that out, but you have to really listen." I spent the next three decades trying to figure out who was a coconut and how to save them and change them into law-abiding citizens.

I had been working there three months when I preached a sermon on taking personal responsibility for crime to which an inmate took an objection. During the sermon the inmate raised his hand and said, "Chaplain, with all due respect, you are preaching in here about a Matthew and a Mark and Luke that lived a long time ago. If you want to get relative (sic) preach about Big Al, Many Soda fats, Icepick, Fat Tony, because they are in here now, and no Matthew or Mark or Luke is in here. Maybe other people put us here, not us."

No one had ever interrupted before, and I knew this guy to be a jitterbug junkie type that was juiced on Meth, so I politely said, "I appreciate your comments and concerns, but let me just get through the sermon and we can have a discussion after the service." I spoke about five seconds and he shook his head, blurted out, "No, my man, I mean if you get relative, (sic) you will preach about why we have to eat lousy food like powdered eggs instead of real eggs, and baloney sandwiches and pea soup for lunch and stuff like that." He went on and on and would not shut up.

The interruption was disturbing me, but I said, "If you will allow me to finish my sermon, we can deal with your concerns afterwards." He started right in again and this time he really let loose for about three or four minutes of inmate complaints, which I call the Inmate Bitch Game. It went on and on about how the Warden would not let him make many phone calls, and officers told him decisions and then took them back, his cell was smelly, his celly was a fool, his cigarettes were stolen and no one would do anything about it, and so on. I stopped him after four minutes and said, "Man, I feel like throwing this Bible at you. " A guy in the back shouted, "DO IT!"

It took about three seconds for me to react, but I threw that *Scofield Reference Bible* right at the junkie and hit him right smack in the head even though he partially blocked the throw with his arms and pages flew everywhere. He was in the second pew so he was real close. He was shocked but started to rise up in the pew and come after me. An ex-Hells Angel's guy sitting behind him said, "Sit down" and stuffed him back down in the pew. A lot of commotion and noise from other inmates ensued and the officer came running in from the library to the small chapel and said, "What is going on in here, Chaplain?" I said, "We are having a lively discussion about the sermon and we are now going to have the benediction." During the benediction, I said to bless us all and help us all to deal with our tempers that sometimes get out of hand." I was off and gone in seconds.

All week long I was on pins and needles and fully expected to get fired for throwing the Bible and hitting an inmate in the head with it. Thursday the Warden called me into his office and said, "Chaplain, you will never believe what these fool inmates told me – they said you threw a Bible and hit one in the head during chapel service on Sunday. Haw Haw Haw, these guys think I will believe anything and he slapped his leg." I said, "Warden there is only one thing. I did throw that Bible at an inmate and hit him in the head and it was (the name of the inmate)."

The Warden looked incredulous. His mouth opened wide and his eyes kind of bugged out. He just looked at me in shock for about

10 seconds. His eyes narrowed, and he said in a low and controlled voice, "I have one question for you, Chaplain. Did he deserve it?"

I said, "Yes sir, he did." He said, "Well, I am not a real religious man, and, in fact, I am a Roaming Catholic." He spelled out R O A M I N G for me so I would get it. "Well, all right then, if he deserved it, I guess you did what you had to do, but by God don't throw any more GD Bibles in my GD Chapel again, you got that Chaplain? I said, "Yes sir." He said, "Damnation," and I left quickly.

I know I should have been fired for that and maybe even sued. It was not Jesus- like behavior, but it was me-like, at the time and at my age. It was not the first or last time I would make a serious mistake in corrections, but it was one of the most "grace-full" responses I ever got from a Warden after such a serious mistake had been made. The Warden had been there 37 years and thought he had seen everything. He did say a week later that if the inmate sued me he would have to let me go. The inmate never sued me but my Hitachi boom box was stolen out of my YMCA office soon after the junkie was released. Word from inside was that the junkie stole it to pay me back.

In those three seconds of hesitation and reaction by impulse I defined my ministry. As the ex-Hell's Angel guy said, "Chaplain, You made your bones that day when you hit that guy in the head with your Bible. The guy is weirded out on speed and has driven us all crazy with his constant jabber and we all thought it was great what you did. You also didn't rat him out when the officer rushed in." Next week there was standing room only in the Chapel but the junkie was not there. He had been released from his short sentence at the jail, much to my relief. I guess I literally had done what they tell you to do in seminary. I had hit him with the Word.

One of the highlights in working as a jail chaplain is working with some really fine volunteers. I started a program from Dr. Milton "Mickey" Burglass, called Thresholds, and it taught inmates decision-making skills they could use to avoid doing crime. Dr. Burglass is a renowned psychiatrist who did a year as a thief in the New Orleans City Jail. He trained our volunteers over an intense weekend and then other volunteers and I trained them further in jail policies. We trained 200 people in the three years I was there. They went into the jail Friday evening, all day Saturday and all day Sunday for a marathon macro-micro group experience with a group of 10 inmates and 12 volunteers.

Some of the most intense experiences of my life occurred in these marathon weekends at the jail. Two volunteers ran the group, and 10 volunteers were paired with individual inmates to teach the problem-solving and decision-making skills to inmates. I am unaware of any research that proves a reduction in crime among Threshold inmates who graduate versus a random control group of inmates who did not participate. But I can tell you that much quality time was spent by well-trained volunteers to try to change some Coconuts into law-abiding citizens. After a particularly intense weekend, we were all in a group singing Harum Bey, which means to work together. Several inmates were crying and volunteers were crying, and I thought to myself, "Jesus Christ would be moved by the love that is in this room right now." I was 27, very naïve, and unrealistically hopeful.

From that weekend, two people met inside the jail and later married. The woman was in seminary at the time and later became a United Methodist Pastor, and the inmate became a friend for many years. Sadly, the inmate resorted to heroin use again about 10 years later, did some burglaries to pay for the drugs and went to prison for a while. He was released and died of liver problems from alcohol a few years later. My friend the pastor influenced many a jail chaplain based on her life experiences. The Lord uses us to transcend the problems of inmates and to come up with our own solutions of dealing with them.

My female jail chapel organist met a woman serving time in jail and allowed the female inmate to live with her family after release from jail (against my pleas to not do this). My organist later left in a lesbian relationship with the ex-inmate, divorced her husband of 17 years, and left the three children as well. Another of my volunteers fell for an inmate motorcycle biker. The biker moved into her house and ran up huge grocery and telephone bills. He kept a powder gun loaded because he was selling hot bikes in parts and pieces from her garage. She kicked him out before he was caught.

I tell these stories because if anyone thinks it is easy to work as a volunteer up front and personal with inmates in city or county jail or state or federal prison, they are sadly mistaken. It is very hard to keep to your own values when the inmate is trying to manipulate you for his or her own ends. Most inmates I have met are more takers than givers, and they have learned to take things from others rather than to earn them. Some tried to get money from volunteers, date their daughters or wives or date the volunteer, get volunteers to smuggle contraband in or out of prison, bring drugs, or alcohol or money in. They routinely asked the volunteers to call lawyers or write to judges on their behalf. I trained my volunteers better than that, but they sometimes would not listen to me. As a result they got burned.

The volunteers transformed that little jail and many an inmate. The jail was not isolated from the community if the community voluntarily entered it for marathon weekends. The intense marathon weekend broke down some of the barriers that inmates exhibit. Teaching the inmates decision-making and problem-solving skills to help them change their lives had a profound effect, which I personally witnessed. The personal one-to-one sessions over the weekend allowed each inmate to dig into his life and see how he could apply decision-making skills rather than operate on impulse. One of my theories about many inmates is that they operate on poor impulse control based on their perception of self as a loser, a drunk, a junkie, a criminal, a tough guy, and so forth. Drugs and alcohol often lower a person's ability to control impulses. Teaching them that they can decide to be different is a huge step and a major change for many of them.

I did make my bones in that county jail but not the way inmates mean. By trial and error and by osmosis with the correctional officers I listened to, I learned what was acceptable and not acceptable in jail. I learned it was life and death in a jail. I was in B cell house tier and locked in when a foolish inmate burned his clothing, pillow and mattress in his cell. We all started yelling FIRE and HELP, but it was precious minutes of a smoked-filled tier that filled our lungs with smoke, and we all could have died. Fortunately, an officer heard our cries and came in and saved us. But I never forgot that helpless feeling. I knew then this was serious business.

In jail I conducted the marriage for three inmates and their wives-to-be. The first two marriages were fine, but the third one was why I never officiated at another marriage of an incarcerated person. The third inmate got out of jail and wanted his new wife to perform sex with animals for him, and when she would not do it he beat her almost to death. I visited her in the hospital and she came by the office when she got out of the hospital. She was beaten so severely you could only see one eye. I realized that though I had conducted the marriage for that inmate, I did not know him; therefore, I had not really counseled the bride and groom enough to know if marriage was a responsible decision for each of them. I felt that the bride should have been given the information about the violence in the inmate's past and should have had an opportunity to have premarital counseling because she had only met him briefly in jail and they did not know each other well enough to get married. As a result I never personally conducted a marriage for any other inmate.

I did only one funeral outside of jail or prison on behalf of a female ex-inmate, but it was a doozy. The lady served time in jail for an alcoholic crime and was released to the community when she got word her father died. She called my office and wanted me to do the funeral up in Lake Hopatcong because she was not religious and I was the only pastor she really knew. When I saw her at the graveside service she wobbled up to me. The smell of scotch almost overwhelmed me when she shook my hand. There were only four of us present at the graveside funeral and we were all standing next to the open grave when I was reading, "Dust to dust . . .," and she swooned, passed out and fell into the open grave.

They just don't tell you what to do in seminary when a person falls into an open grave at a funeral. I had to take off my black preacher's robe and get down into the grave. With the help of an elderly man who I think was her brother, I lifted that dead weight of a passed-out woman. We flopped her out of the grave an inch at a time and got some water and threw it on her three times to revive her. We found a chair for her and I finished the graveside service. I told a seminary professor that story, and he told me I had been disaster-proofed by that incident and nothing like that would happen to me in my career. He was wrong as later events would show.

One of the hardest things about being a jail chaplain is finding funding. Unless you are paid by the city or county, you are a community-based chaplaincy and always looking for funding support. I had 108 Protestant and Catholic churches that supported the Morris County Chaplaincy Council. I spoke about 50 times a year to various churches about the jail ministry and that took a great deal of time. Fortunately, in my third year I won a $100,000 LEEA grant through New Jersey's State Law Enforcement Planning Agency, and my funding problems were solved. If I had stayed, I was planning to ask the county to fund the chaplaincy. There is, however, plenty of freedom in being an outside agency that you give up if employed by the county government, which in New Jersey was the Board of Chosen Freeholders.

More than three years in jail chaplaincy I learned about inmate needs. They needed toothbrushes and toilet items, and they were poor and functioned at about a 6th grade level of education. About 75% of them had drug or alcohol problems. I learned that I could not save every inmate. Many were going to be career criminals no matter what I did as preacher, counselor or teacher. In a few months I learned that inmate needs will swamp you and your ability to provide resources. A hundred times a day on the tiers—they would ask me to do something for them. That is when it dawned on me that *I would not rob an inmate of the victory of solving his own problems.* This was a key awareness that I kept with me for the rest of my career. It would go something like this.

> INMATE: Chaplain, will you write a letter to the judge for me on my behalf?
>
> ME: I am sorry I cannot do that, but you can write the letter to the Judge from your own perspective.
>
> INMATE: Naw—the Judge won't listen to me
>
> ME: Who knows you better than you and you can write him what you want him to know?
>
> INMATE: Chaplain, listen man—that was a great sermon you gave about helping people. Will you call my lawyer

for me and tell him to call my wife to hear my alibi for the crime

ME: I am sorry I cannot do that, but you can call your wife or write your wife and tell her to call your lawyer.

INMATE: Chaplain, will you lend me some money because I owe my cellmate for cigarettes and he may hurt me?

ME: I am sorry but I cannot give you money, which is contraband, but you can earn it in your work detail or call family or friends and have some money sent in to your commissary account. If you have been threatened, you can tell the lieutenant and he can put you in Administrative Segregation for protection, or if you are actually telling me you have been threatened, I have to tell the Lt. myself for your own protection. If the inmate confirmed it, I would get him in Seg for his own protection.

If you rescue an inmate and do for him what he can do for himself, then they will come back to you to be rescued again and again. When the inmates were on the outside doing their crime, they were the persecutor and had power over their victims. They were robbing, raping, ripping off some vulnerable victims and they had the power. When the tables turned and, they got caught, prosecuted, convicted, sentenced and incarcerated they start playing the victim because they are in prison and being controlled by the prison system. They lost all their power. Then they look for chaplains, psychologists and caseworkers, or counselors (whom they refer to as "easy marks") to rescue them or get some sympathy for their victimization in prison. This is sympathy they never showed to their victims but they want it for themselves. They play poor helpless inmate to the hilt. They play "poor me" and "born to lose" and "I am no good" and "bad to the bone" messages in their head all day long to gain sympathy and manipulate others for their own ends.

Some inmates have been victimized by beatings and abuse, molested as children, subjected to drugs, and alcohol abuse. Some have serious mental health problems and have been diagnosed with serious mental disorders. Some of their parents were criminals and they introduced them to a life of crime. About 75% of the inmates I met had drug and or alcohol abuse problems. Many inmates had a string of prior convictions. Does that excuse their criminal behavior? No, but it does explain it. I always thought it was important to know and understand the history and the crime background of who I was dealing with in jail. It could save my life as well as others, by knowing that information. For example, I never walked up to an organized-crime hit man, or any inmate for that matter, and said something disrespectful or demeaning to him or to other inmates. As they say in jail, "Paybacks are hell."

This persecutor to victim, victim to rescuer game, known as the Karpman Drama Triangle in Transactional Analysis, plays out in prison on a daily basis. Chaplains are expected to be rescuers and easy marks in jail, so inmates usually try to play them first. Early I had to figure out how far I would go for an inmate. I wanted some independent verification of facts before I would act. I ascertained whether or not the inmate was telling the truth by checking on the story to see if it were true before I would act.

In the jail we had an incident in which a whole tier of inmates disliked an officer they thought was racist. They decided to rig the TV electrical cord to the bars the officer touched when unlocking the outside tier door. As soon as he touched it an electrical shock went through his body and scared him greatly. They all laughed and jeered at him while he was being shocked. That night after the incident, the officers on night duty thought it was terrible that the officer was shocked electrically by inmates and could have been hurt seriously. The inmate story was that a few of the night shift officers retaliated and brought in gloves and rolls of quarters. Then they took each inmate out of the cell one by one and hit him in the hair part of the head and stomach where the marks would not show. The next day I walked the tiers and one of the inmates comes up with a broken nose and dried blood under his nostrils. I asked him what happened and he said, "Last night the bulls dragged me out of my cell and hit me on the top of my head with gloves and I looked up and they broke my nose." I did not know what to believe, but every other inmate on the same tier told me the same story, and some showed me bruises on their stomachs or sides, but no other facial bruises could be seen.

I asked an officer I respected about it, but he knew nothing. I decided to write it up and give this alleged story to the Warden. I went over to the office and typed up what was said, who said it, and the marks I saw. I had to go to the doctor that afternoon, so the next morning I walked in to the jail with my report, and investigators for the prosecutor's office were all over the place talking to inmates. A reporter for the *Morris County Daily Record* had gone through the day before in a tour of the jail right after I was walking the tiers, and he had been slipped a note by an inmate who said several of the night shift officers beat him up last night after dragging him out of his cell. After the investigation, the prosecutor convened a grand jury, and I was asked along with many others to go there and tell what I knew. They made the decision before I was called in to the jury room. I gave my oral report to the foreman of the grand jury when he stepped out to tell me they had made a decision. I stated I had been told this story about beatings by inmates, but I had seen none of the beatings actually happen. He asked me if inmates could have had fights among themselves on the tier and then told this story about the officers, which is what the night shift officers claimed to be true. I said I did not know what was true or not, but allegedly an officer was almost electrocuted by inmates and then allegedly some officers pummeled some inmates. While neither behavior is morally right or legal, it seems to me to be "dead steven even" in the jail right now. It is hard to know who to believe here. A civil rights violation is very serious in a jail and needs to be taken seriously. In this case it was a 50-50 standoff as far as the evidence went.

The foreman said, "Thank you, chaplain. There will be no more questions." The grand jury returned a no bill on the indictment. I think they saw it as a standoff in which inmates said one thing and officers said the opposite and there was no actual proof for the inmates, so they let it drop.

I want to talk about jail rules. Early, I fought the struggle between grace and the law every day in the joint. Eventually I received a copy of the jail rules to read and got some sort of basic training on the

Rules and Operating Procedures and policies of the jail. My basic training was by the captain, "Here, Chap, read the rules and don't break em." Sometimes I felt like a cop and had to bust an inmate for misconduct, or breaking the rules, or even the law. If I failed to do this, I would be covering up the misconduct and threatening the entire staff's security. I had to be on the staff's side about rules, obey them myself, and make sure the inmates under my authority and in my chapel area obeyed the same rules.

So I tried never to be caught between the staff and inmates because inmates are always breaking the rules. That is why they are inmates—they break laws to get there. If I functioned as a *staff* chaplain, inmates saw me as a cop. If I worked as an *inmate's* chaplain, staff did not trust me. Basically, I straddled the fence of trying to be pastoral to staff and inmates alike and to be fair, caring and honest to all. If I saw a wrong, I had to report it, and if I did something wrong myself, I had to admit it. I did not make the mistake of lying about what I did, because I could be fired for lying to a supervisor during an investigation. If I messed up, I fessed up.

When I did something wrong, it could be handled by my evaluation being negative that year. I was never reprimanded or suspended. If I had lied, I would run the risk of being fired for lying. In addition, if staff learned that I lied, even if I were not fired, they know they cannot trust me or my word. I was a staff chaplain more than I was an inmate's chaplain, but I did try to be both as best I could.

People have heard of a shank mentioned on TV shows, but until you see a writing pen ground into a sharp point, or a razor on the end of a toothbrush, or a metal plate sanded into a sharp edge, you don't really know all the variations of the word *shank*. Part of my job was to go around in the jail chapel and make sure no illegal contraband like drugs or weapons such as shanks or garrotes were in my area. If I found one, I turned it in to the officers.

Also, I will never forget a young officer who first told me about coded messages as an item of contraband. He said, "Chap, the inmates in here use coded messages about drug talk and they will ask you to call a family member and deliver the message for them. You could be putting a hit on someone or authorizing a gang member to sell some cocaine in the code you take out of here and deliver to a family member on the outside." From that day on I was very careful not to deliver any kind of message to a family member that came from an inmate. I asked the inmate to deliver messages himself by phone or in writing. The exception to this is when a death occurred and I had to deliver the news to an inmate and talk to his family. My strong suggestion is to always verify the death as I had more than one irate ex-wife call and say a death occurred in order to get the inmate to call her and pay her back alimony.

    I drove a Honda 350 motorcycle to work at the jail and wore a clerical collar, jeans and motorcycle boots. We could not afford a second car when I was in seminary or the first two years afterwards. Back then, in '70 to '73 my hair was pretty long. The warden affectionately called me the Hoodlum Priest. He liked me because I brought in volunteers whom he liked, and he got a lot more recognition in the community because I asked him to go with me to speak to some churches about the needs of the jail and about the jail ministry. Before I came, he said the jail had been pretty isolated from public awareness or volunteers.

    I counseled hundreds of inmates in my daily walks of the tiers, and I preached about 150 sermons to them, gave them communion once a month, married three, did a funeral for one, baptized four, did the Sinner's Prayer and brought several to accept Christ as their Savior. I did not have a way to know if I really made a difference because I did not track the ex-inmates I counseled. I have to trust in the ways of the Lord and say that if they genuinely accepted Christ, then their lives and behavior will change and they will not resort again to crime, or not as much crime, or less serious crimes. I did six marathon weekends with 12 volunteers and 10 inmates at each weekend event. Two of us ran the group sessions, and the other volunteers did one-to-one counseling in between groups. Each marathon was a powerful and emotional experience and I would not take anything for them. It changed the inmates and volunteers and me. I know this because I was with them each marathon and it changed me in a positive way, so I assume it affected them in the same way.

    A colleague chaplain asked me a question that puts it all into perspective: "How many inmates that you met in jail would you trust if your life depended on their word and their truth?" I can think of two. He also asked me how many I would trust to marry my daughter. I could not think of one. It then dawned on me that I can love someone in Christ, but not like him, or more specifically, not like the behavior that put him in jail. When you know that inmate in front of you raped an elderly senile woman or stole from a retarded boy or molested a three-year-old girl, it is hard to like that person. I can pray earnestly for his soul and that he accept Christ and know the love and joy that comes from walking with Christ, but I do not have to be so naive to think that the same person I am praying for in that moment would not hesitate to burglarize my home if he were strung out on drugs and needed money to pay for the drugs.

I had a case of Christian Ethics 101 real soon in the jail. During a weekend marathon one of the pairings of inmate-to-female-volunteer involved a gang member, which I will call Heller, though that's not his real name. Heller was crying in the group and asking for forgiveness for all his wrongs he had done. He cried in the one-to-one sessions with the female volunteer. He said he accepted Christ for the first time in the group, but I was a bit suspicious as he said he had just accepted Christ to me a month earlier when I counseled him on the wing (the segregation area he was in for fighting with another inmate)

Heller was officially in jail for stealing a watch from a 14-year-old mentally retarded boy, but he had spilled his real story to me that he had killed someone and would be indicted next month for murder. He had joined the gang based on obeying an order to beat a young boy senseless and broke the boy's collarbone in three places. As he talked about the gang his eyes would light up with pride.

Heller said he and 17 others raped a girl to help her become a gang mama, which she later became. He said he was in the back seat of a car with a shotgun trained on the head of a gang leader's wife, and his gang buddy had a shotgun on the gang leader, who was driving the car. Heller said they hit a bump and the shotgun discharged accidentally and he blew the woman's head off. Immediately, the other gang buddy had to shoot the gang leader as well. After being shot, the leader, who was driving, wrecked the car, but both Heller and his buddy in the back seat escaped. Both victims were shot dead.

The female volunteer was taken with the inmate's crying, sincerity, asking for forgiveness and Heller asked her to write a letter to the judge for him. Of course, Heller let her think she was writing a letter to the judge about the crime of theft of a watch from a young boy and not any of the more serious offenses. Because all the other information came to me during a visit with a group of inmates in Segregation (Seg), I could not tell the female volunteer about the violence of breaking collarbones, gang raping a woman or double homicide. The volunteer came to me and asked if she could write a letter to the judge on Heller's behalf. I said no because that was against policy, but I would ask the Warden if I could write a letter on Heller's behalf. The volunteer understood and said okay. I did write such a letter, showed it to the Warden, and he approved it to go to the judge. It said something like this based on my memory,

Dear Judge,

I understand that inmate Heller has recently been convicted and sentenced for a double murder in Morris County. With all due respect, I think he should serve whatever maximum sentence you and the jury deem appropriate. I do, however, sincerely pray for his soul.

Sincerely,
Chaplain Bruce Cook

Forgiveness is not forgetting or condoning. It is not letting someone off for his misdeeds. Heller should pay for his crimes and was given a life sentence. As chaplains we can offer him the forgiveness that comes from genuine and contrite repentance that is available to all of us as sinners. God is the only one who can judge Heller's true repentance. I still pray for his soul. I pray for the victims of his crimes and their eternal souls as well and their families. I never want to lose even one soul to the devil.

The experience of a jail chaplain is not all so serious. There is a lot of homespun humor in a jail. We had an inmate who had been drunk and tried to rob a bank by demand note, and the note he used was written on the back side of his own deposit slip. A slim burglar tried to enter a chimney to burglarize a house and got stuck in the chimney. One drunk robbed a convenience store with a pocket knife that fell apart when he pushed the blade out. When the cops came, the store owner said, "Your cab is here." The drunk got in the police car and told the "cabbie" officer to take him to his home address as the store owner was rude to him. One of the inmate cooks told me what they did to pea soup, or what they called *pee soup*, and I never ate jail food again. Inmates on the tier played poker and the loser had to drink an eight-ounce glass of water. A poor poker player got so full of water he had to be taken to the hospital but not before he peed all over himself and the tier floor. The staff was always teasing each other about something and sometimes teased the inmates. In such a confined setting you need to laugh to displace some tension. The humor needs to be funny but not so insulting that it causes more tension.

An outstanding example of voluntarism in the jail was Grace. I will call her Amazing Grace. She was very wealthy, and she heard me speak at a local church and signed up to be a jail volunteer to teach Dr. Burglass' Thresholds Program of decision-making and problem-solving skills to inmates over a marathon week-end in the jail. The first thing that happened in her case was my organist, Bruce Talbert, wanted to screen her out of the program. He said she was too judgmental. I said, "Bruce, do you think this 50 year old lady is really going to hurt any of these inmates with her strong opinions?"

So Grace went in for a weekend and I placed her with Icepick (not his real name), an organized-crime hit man. I will never forget seeing her standing up in Icepick's face and jabbing her finger repeatedly in his chest and saying, "When are you going to stop making decisions that hurt people and start helping people?" I bet Icepick remembers that lady, too. I doubt too many have spoken to him like that and lived.

What I remember her for most was not her strong opinions but her bravery. She volunteered to read Scripture on Sundays in the jail chapel service, and on a particular Sunday the Warden met us in front of the key room as we entered. He said, "Chaplain, I don't think it is a good idea to go in to the Jail and do the service this morning. We have some snitch information that they are going to take hostages in the service. But it is your call and I will leave it up to you."

I said, "Warden, that is my job and I am going in and I don't show fear. Never ever! But I will not ask my substitute organist, at that time a woman named Judy, or Grace, the volunteer, to go in with me."

Grace said rather abruptly, "Wait just one minute, Reverend Cook. If you are going in, I am going in and that is the end of it, as far as I am concerned." The organist looked less certain but also agreed to go in. We all signed a brief statement that the Warden had prepared saying we had been warned about the situation and decided to go in anyway. I think he was concerned about Grace's team of lawyers coming after him if he didn't.

When we got to the chapel in the opening prayer, I did something I am not sure was smart, but it worked just the same. In the prayer I said we had been told that some inmates were going to take hostages and we decided to come to the chapel anyway because we served God and did not fear man. I heard later that the two inmates who were going to take hostages that Sunday morning decided not to do it after what was said. There were also four officers in the back of the chapel instead of the usual one who stayed in the library next to the chapel. That was just in case. It is one thing to shoot a lamb by surprise and altogether another issue to shoot one who walks up to you and asks to be sacrificed.

Jesus was like that self-surrendering lamb. We tried to be like Him in this incident. It took guts to go in after being told they may try to take you hostage and even more courage from female volunteers. The women had more to lose if raped and it was not their paid job to go in as it was for me. True heroines in my opinion!

One of the things we started was an after-care program in the community, and we worked with ex-inmates to get jobs, places to live, and develop relationships with churches and law abiding citizens. It was tough and we often encountered a lot of resistance to employ ex-offenders, and I never blamed the public for the way they felt. But if we don't offer ex-inmates some form of job, they will resort to crime to pay the bills because that is what they know. We offered an aftercare program to teach problem-solving skills in a church in the county, but it was so difficult to get ex-inmates to attend regularly that we had to cancel it.

What did I learn in this job that could help another chaplain or a future volunteer in a jail?

1. Wait to verify a statement from an inmate before you believe it to be true. Rescuers can stay away from this job or fight the urge to rescue. Enable but don't rescue.
2. Don't rob an inmate of the victory of solving his own problems.
3. Don't let the "takers" take anything illegal from you, and don't bring anything into the jail or out of the jail for the inmate. That includes a written or verbal message, which is actually contraband. "Tell the boys to tell my three girls I will send them $10 each," may mean: "Sell three kilos of cocaine for $10,000 each."
4. Train staff and volunteers well and you will have fewer problems in a jail, but you will still have problems and should pray for some degree of grace.
5. You will never know for certain how many inmates you helped, but if they genuinely accepted Christ, it is one less soul the devil will take. If you just helped one and that one did not rape or rob or kill your loved one or someone else's, then it was all worthwhile. You will never know how many crimes were avoided by a changed life who accepted Christ.
6. Inmates can be taught good decision-making skills that will help them solve problems, but unless they change their values they will just be a smarter criminal.

**Some Statistics from the Bureau of Justice Statistics:
An Overview of the Jail and Prison Problem in the USA**

Summary Findings: Jails are locally-operated correctional facilities that confine persons before or after adjudication. Inmates sentenced to jail usually have a sentence of a year or less, but jails also incarcerate persons in a wide variety of other categories.

Jail Facilities

- At midyear 2008, 785,556 inmates were held in the nation's local jails, up from 780,174 at midyear 2007.

- In 2008, jails reported adding 14,911 beds during the previous 12 months, bringing the total rated capacity to 828,413.

- 95% of the rated capacity was occupied at mid-year 2008. On June 30, 2008 local jails were operating 5% below their rated capacity.

- From 2000 to 2008, the number of jail inmates per 100,000 U.S. residents rose from 226 to 258.

- From midyear 2007 to midyear 2008, the 12-month increase of 0.7% in the jail population the smallest annual rate of growth in 27 years.

Jail Population

- Almost nine out of every ten jail inmates were adult males. However, the number of adult females in jail increased faster than males.

- Between 1990 and 2008, the number of Hispanic jail inmates increased at a faster average annual rate of growth (4.5%) than white (3.8%) and black inmates (3.3%).

- Blacks were three times more likely than Hispanics and five times more likely than whites to be in jail.

On June 30, 2008

- 2,310,984 prisoners were held in federal or state prisons or in local jails—an increase of 0.8% from yearend 2007, less than the average annual growth of 2.4% from 2000-2007.

- 1,540,805 sentenced prisoners were under state or federal jurisdiction.

- There were an estimated 509 sentenced prisoners per 100,000 U.S. residents—up from 506 at yearend 2007.

- The number of women under the jurisdiction of state or federal prison authorities increased 1.2% from yearend 2007, reaching 115,779, and the number of men rose 0.7%, and totaling 1,494,805.

At midyear 2008, there were 4,777 black male inmates per 100,000 U.S. residents being held in state or federal prison and local jails, compared to 1,760 Hispanic male inmates per 100,000 U.S. residents and 727 white male inmates per 100,000 U.S. residents.

In 2005 there were an estimated 687,700 state prisoners serving time for a violent offense. State prisons also held an estimated 248,900 property offenders and 253,300 drug offenders.

Most Serious Offense Percent of Sentenced

State inmates	1995	2005
Violent	47%	53%
Property	23%	19%
Drug	22%	20%
Public-order	9%	8%

Probationers include adult offenders whom courts place on community supervision generally in lieu of incarceration. Parolees include those adults conditionally released to community supervision whether by parole board decision or by mandatory conditional release after serving a prison term. They are subject to being returned to jail or prison for rule violations or other offenses.

- At year-end 2007, over 5.1 million adult men and women were supervised in the community, either on probation or parole. More than 8 in 10 were on probation (4,293,163), while less than 2 in 10 were on parole (826,097).

- About 1 in every 45 adults in the U.S. was supervised in the community, either on probation or parole, at yearend 2007.

- The total community supervision population grew by 104,100 offenders during 2007. While the parole population (up 3.3%) increased at a faster pace than the probation population (up 1.8%) during the year, probation accounted for three-quarters (77,800) of the growth in the number of offenders under community supervision.

- During 2007, a total of 1,248,337 parolees were at-risk of being re-incarcerated, which included those under parole supervision on January 1 or who entered parole during the year. Of these parolees, about 16% were returned to incarceration in 2007.

Source: Bureau of Justice Statistics: http://www.ojp.usdoj.gov/bjs

Facts about the Morris County Jail and the Thresholds Program

As the county jail chaplain, I looked at volunteer programs across the country suitable for county jails, and happened onto the Thresholds Program. I was looking for one that would fit a small 100-man jail and that could be delivered quickly; because the turnover rate was so high (average sentence was only 45 days). There were not many counseling programs to select. There were more than 4000 jails in 1970 and many had no programs at all. There were 11% work release, 10% educational, 9% counseling, 7% Alcoholics Anonymous, and 20% classified as "other" programs, usually religious programs according to the LEEA National Jail Census.

I heard about a successful program that operated in the Bucks County Jail in 1969. Its originator, Dr. Milton E. "Mickey" Burglass, served a year as a thief in the New Orleans Parish Prison. Mickey encountered the Imaginal Education program in the parish prison, which came from the Ecumenical Institute in Chicago. It changed his life and he later modified it into the Thresholds Program for use in jails and prisons. Dr. Burglass said many times it was not "his" program but was "our" program to modify as we needed. He is now a psychiatrist renown for treating addictions.

The basic assumption of the Thresholds Program is that inmates are not sick or mentally ill but are impulsive and make poor choices with a lack of impulse control, resulting in crime. The way they behave becomes the way they see themselves. Their behavior leads to or derives from their self-image, and the one reinforces the other. In my opinion an inmate's self-image can be of one who thinks he can do anything (Superman image) but can barely read or write. It can be of one who thinks he can do nothing (Victim image) and is "born to lose."

Because the self-image is negative, self-destructive and self–defeating, the decisions an inmate makes are consistent within the way he sees himself. Therefore, the Thresholds Program seeks to teach him in a didactic group and individual series of volunteer-led sessions how to make decisions "with the least minimal regret and the most positive outcome." The program teaches him how to define the situation, set and achieve realistic goals with specific strategies and tactics, even down to the detail of making a daily list of activities to be completed in order to achieve the stated goals. By looking at all the possibilities and evaluating the best ones, a person can make and implement a decision that is positive. The program is encouraging and positive in its belief that the inmate can take responsibility (response ability or ability to respond) for his own life and turn it around in a positive manner. Dr. Burglass is a prime example of one who did just that.

I modified Thresholds into a 20-hour marathon weekend that included six group or macro sessions, and matched 12 volunteers with 12 inmates in six individual or micro sessions. The macro-micro approach was conducted in sequence and what was taught in the group session was then reinforced in the individual session that followed. I also started an Ongoing Program in the jail, or six sessions that met weekly after the marathon weekend to reinforce what was learned. Then there was an after-care component, which met in a church on a weekly basis, but it never really was successful because some inmates did not want to keep meeting with other inmates in the community, and some could not because of conditions of parole or probation that prohibited them from association with felons. About 108 volunteers were trained for this Thresholds program, and in two years they spent 500 hours in the jail counseling inmates through the program.

A psychologist, Ms. Crane Groesbeck, who worked for the Morris County Sheriff, conducted a brief study of 158 non-inmates and 118 inmates of the county jail, and concluded that inmates were 16% higher than the control group in seeing themselves as internally controlled (Superman Image) and 16% higher seeing themselves as controlled by outside forces (Victim Image) based on the scores of the Rotter Internal Locus of Felt Control tests. I never saw the actual study or learned how the non-inmates were selected.

At the time, back in 1970, this was a small jail with a largely white, young, and uneducated inmate population with drugs and alcohol the main offenses. I needed a program that could be delivered to that population without losing half of my participants because they had been let out before the program ended. The Thresholds

Program fit the bill and was an excellent way to teach inmates they could be responsible decision makers and problem solvers.

The main criticism I had of Thresholds was that if the inmates did not change their values, they just became smarter criminals. It was my belief back then, and it still is, that to change their values required a religious belief in God and acceptance of the teachings of Jesus Christ. Then an alcoholic became a redeemed alcoholic and not just a recovered alcoholic. As such, he is claimed by Christ and the need and desire for alcohol or drugs, what inmates called "the taste," could go away as well as the alcoholic lifestyle. The Christian lifestyle replaces it. The Thresholds Program is value free and teaches problem solving and decision making, and leaves the decision up to the inmate whether he chooses to believe in God.

The Thresholds Program is still operating 30 years after I found it. It is very active in jails and prisons in the Connecticut, Pennsylvania, Delaware, upstate New York area, and is in the Georgia Prisons. The Bureau of Prisons also has a Thresholds Program, which is a different model. (See www.thresholdsdelco.org for more information.) It can be replicated in a number of jails and prisons, and is an excellent program.

The Morris County Jail today is a new facility built in 2000 to serve 528 inmates and averages 330 inmates per day. It was one of 160 jails among 3,213 jails nationwide to receive American Corrections Association accreditation and is one of the top jails in the country, receiving a score of 100% in meeting 57 mandatory standards according to the Star-Ledger newspaper article by Matt Dowling on May 13, 2009.

The Main Scriptural Basis for Helping Those in Prison:
Here is what God says in Matthew 25:31-46 (Eugene Petersons' *The Message*):

[31-33]"When he finally arrives, blazing in beauty and all his angels with him, the Son of Man will take his place on his glorious throne. Then all the nations will be arranged before him and he will sort the people out, much as a shepherd sorts out sheep and goats, putting sheep to his right and goats to his left.

[34-36]"Then the King will say to those on his right, 'Enter, you who are blessed by my Father! Take what's coming to you in this kingdom. It's been ready for you since the world's foundation. And here's why:
 I was hungry and you fed me,
 I was thirsty and you gave me a drink,
 I was homeless and you gave me a room,
 I was shivering and you gave me clothes,
 I was sick and you stopped to visit,
 I was in prison and you came to me.'
[37-40]"Then those 'sheep' are going to say, 'Master, what are you talking about? When did we ever see you hungry and feed you, thirsty and give you a drink? And when did we ever see you sick or in prison and come to you?' Then the King will say, 'I'm telling the solemn truth: Whenever you did one of these things to someone overlooked or ignored, that was me—you did it to me.'
[41-43]"Then he will turn to the 'goats,' the ones on his left, and say, 'Get out, worthless goats! You're good for nothing but the fires of hell. And why? Because—
I was hungry and you gave me no meal,
 I was thirsty and you gave me no drink,
 I was homeless and you gave me no bed,
 I was shivering and you gave me no clothes,
 Sick and in prison, and you never visited.'
[44] "Then those 'goats' are going to say, 'Master, what are you talking about? When did we ever see you hungry or thirsty or homeless or shivering or sick or in prison and didn't help?'
[45] "He will answer them, 'I'm telling the solemn truth: Whenever you failed to do one of these things to someone who was being overlooked or ignored, that was me—you failed to do it to me.'
[46] "Then those 'goats' will be herded to their eternal doom, but the 'sheep' to their eternal reward."

CHAPTER 2

THE FEDERAL PRISON CHAP

Being a federal prison chaplain is very different from being a local jail chaplain. They train you at the Federal Law Enforcement Training Course in Glynco, Georgia for three weeks. The Bureau of Prisons (BOP) trains you in Institution and Familiarization training within a few weeks of starting on the job. They are a policy-driven agency, so it your obligation to learn and memorize the policy. There is a great deal of POLICY. You have to be credentialed by your ecclesiastical body and endorsed by them to be hired as a federal prison chaplain. You have to be under 37 years of age or transfer in from another federal law enforcement agency. Exceptions can be made for hard-to-place chaplains, including Roman Catholic priests, Muslim imams, Jewish rabbis, and so forth, to waive the age requirement.

I was 42 when I transferred in as a federal prison chaplain, GS12-step 10, from the US Parole Commission in which I had been a parole hearing examiner, GS 14-step 7. Parole was being abolished and moved the Regional Office to Washington, D.C. I did not want to disrupt my wife's retirement plans in Georgia, and I did not want to live in expensive Washington, D.C. I took a large pay cut for the next nine years in which I served as a staff chaplain at the U.S. Penitentiary and Federal Prison Camp in Atlanta, Georgia. I worked three days at the Camp and two at the Pen almost every week and sometimes had to work all week at the Pen to fill in.

This was a cold call. A duty, but only sometimes was it a love of a job. God was still in The Call, but I had heard a great number of parole hearings by then and it had changed me. I was not nearly as naïve or vulnerable to inmate games. I did not want to avoid the Call and be a "goat herded to eternal doom." I knew Jesus was in that prison and I would meet Him there. He would help me through it and be walking right alongside me every step of the way.

It was not a wise thing to do to transfer from being a federal parole examiner to federal prison chaplain, as I had given many federal prisoners a reason to dislike me. When I recommended against paroling some of them and maxed them out or did not parole them as soon as they wanted. I knew this was a "life or death fight against the Devil and all his angels," but that God's words are an indispensable weapon. I wrapped myself in His armor every day I went into that prison and was never harmed. Thanks be to God! I prayed Paul's prayer in Ephesians: "Pray that I will know what to say and have the courage to say it at the right time, telling the mystery to one and all, the Message that I, jailbird preacher that I am, am responsible for getting out" (Ephesians 6:10-20 *The Message* by Eugene Peterson).

The two chaplains that were there already in the Atlanta Federal Penitentiary had been taken hostage three years earlier in the Cuban Hostage crisis in 1987. They were both fine men and true heroes for the way they carried themselves as chaplains and the heroic way they dealt with being a hostage. The Catholic priest and Presbyterian chaplain both were told by the Cubans that they could leave as hostages and exit the institution for their safety. The priest said he would be the last one out and he would be carrying the cross as he walked out. He said he would stay to help them as a Spanish-speaking go between. That proved very helpful because the Cuban inmates trusted the priest. Both chaplains stayed and ministered to staff and inmates alike for 11 days, and there were almost a hundred of them taken hostage. It is one thing to say you are a chaplain and a man of God, but it is another thing to prove it when tested. They both passed the test when they decided to stay because they could have been signing their death warrant by staying. The Cubans were armed with homemade knives and machetes, and if rushed by the FBI, some staff could have been killed in the melee. It was an honor and a privilege to serve with Chaplain Russ Mabry and Father Ray Dowling. I mention them by name because in my opinion they were both heroes.

When I showed up as a newly hired chaplain, Chaplain Mabry and Father Dowling were both very tired of running all over the prison and were in need of some relief. There were almost 2,750 inmates needing their attention, and they were worn out (500 at the Camp, 750 at the Detention Center Unit and 1500 at the Pen). When I started there, one chaplain took two weeks off, and as soon as he got back, the other took two weeks off. I was alone a lot in the chapel in the Pen for the first month.

The first inmate to try to play me as a fish was a D.C. Black, a gang member out of Lorton in D.C. I will call him Screwdriver. When I was alone, he walked into the chaplain's office behind the desk and laid down a large brown bag of cassette tapes. He told me the other chaplains let him store the tapes there because he uses them to play background to sing in the choir on Sunday morning services. He asked if I minded if he left it there, and I said I did not. When he left I went over and looked into the bag. Sure enough, there were cassette tapes. I had not seen the bag there before and something made me suspicious, so I pulled all the tapes out of the bag and there was a screwdriver and a garrote, a wire an assassin tightens around a neck to strangle a victim.

I took the bag over to the lieutenant (LT) and said Screwdriver had left it in my office. I asked the LT if he wanted me to write the shot (misconduct report) or wanted to do it himself, and he said he would take care of it. The screwdriver found in the bag was a hazardous tool that can be used for escape or as a weapon and the garrote was a murder weapon. Inmates are not allowed to have possession of cassette tapes, which can be used as recording devices, and the tapes are supposed to be used only in the chapel. Screwdriver was locked up six months in Seg and came out. I saw him on the mail bag repair work detail and he said, "Man, you ain't no kind of chaplain. You had me locked up." I said, "Not true, Man, you ain't no kind of inmate. You had yourself locked up by trying to fool a poor old chaplain by hiding escape tools."

A week went by, and inmate Screwdriver was walking down the rear corridor to his cell block with a cassette tape in his shirt pocket. The Corridor Officer asked him what he was doing with that item in his possession. Screwdriver said calmly, "Chaplain Cook lets me have these tapes to play in the choir in Chapel." It should be mentioned here that to my knowledge Screwdriver never sang in the chapel. The officer called me in the chapel, and I gave him the background about the screwdriver and garrote and the inmate being in Seg for the same thing for six months. The officer took him by the ear during count and marched him all the way from D cellhouse to Seg for 30 days for lying to a staff member and having possession of an unauthorized item. Screwdriver put the word out that I was a cop and for awhile I did not have any inmates trying to play me.

It is not easy for a chaplain to punish an inmate further by having him locked up in Seg, yet it is absolutely necessary for the security and good order of the institution. Lack of diligence on my part or lack of will to hold an inmate accountable for his actions could result in the inmate escaping or killing someone.

During an after-incident investigation it would come out anyway that the screwdriver tool and garrote were being hidden in the chaplain's office under my very nose and I might lose my job. I also found another inmate hiding stock transactions in the sacristy (a locked and secure closet where we kept communion material), and it had been there for months. The inmate was a white collar offender, and to keep the "tough guy" inmates off him he was advising them to buy and sell stocks to make money while in prison. We had him reprimanded for operating a business in prison. Plus, he could have been killed if the stock transactions went south and inmates lost a lot of money.

A female drug counselor, the wife of a police officer, was pregnant and she worked in the chapel area in the evenings during her drug program. An inmate who was on parole for rape and did another rape on parole was in her class. After class he waited until the other inmates left, and grabbed his crotch and said, "I know what you want and what you need and I can give it to you big time." She got scared and did nothing, but she did tell her husband. He asked her to quit the job and she had been with the BOP for five years. She called me the next day to tell me she would not be coming back to work, and the evening slots were now open in the chapel until she could be replaced. She told me of the inmate threat. I listened and asked her if there was any way she could write a shot for that inmate. She said she could not do that because she had resigned and would not be back.

I went to the captain and said I wanted to have an inmate predator removed from the Pen and transferred. He asked if I would write a "shot" about it and I said I could not as it was hearsay and I did not witness it. I said he could call the drug counselor at home to verify it, but he said," No problem, Chap, he will be in a new zip code tomorrow and he was." Five years went by and the inmate popped back up on the yard in the Atlanta Pen. He told me he went to Lompoc, got kicked out of there, then went to Lewisburg and got kicked out of there, and now he is Atlanta again. I just looked at him and said, "You should not threaten women with your kind of record. If you do, it will be a short stay."

Never, ever, show fear. Never! Take care of business. Write a shot when the behavior demands it. Failure to do so is enabling bad inmate behavior. If we are about the job of correcting behavior or encouraging rehabilitation (whatever that term means today), we have to model good behavior that we expect. Be fair but firm. Punish the bad and reward the good. Remember to show grace and Christian love in all actions. Sometimes real authentic love is tough love. By the way, did I mention I visited Seg and offered to pray with and for every inmate I had locked up there? I only locked up about four inmates, as I recall, but always for good cause. Sometimes they prayed with me in Seg.

I trained a lot of officers and staff during Institution and Familiarization at the Pen. Many were young and brand new to corrections, so I told them a story that helped to orient them to prison life. It goes like this:

An inmate goes up to a newly hired officer who is still on probation and tells the officer his (the inmate's) wife is dying of cancer and the inmate needs to mail a letter to her at the house of an aunt who does not have a phone. He asks the officer if he can borrow one of the stamps from the officer's wallet, and he says he sees the officer pull out several stamps from his wallet earlier. It is too late to get to commissary and to buy the stamps, and he already asked all his cell block buddies and they have no stamps. It will be terrible if he cannot tell his wife he loves her in a letter and she dies beforehand. The officer sympathizes and thinks it will not harm anything to give him one small insignificant stamp, and so he does. The officer thinks it would be terrible if his own wife were dying and he wasn't able to get word to her that he loved her.

The next day the inmate comes up to the officer and says, "Icepick saw you give me a stamp and that is an item of contraband. He wants to get out of here and get to a lower security place and he said he will turn you in unless you bring in some nice stationary from home and he can use it to write his honey." The officer cannot sleep at night and worries about being fired and what would his wife think if he loses his job so he brings in some stationary and gives it to Icepick. Then Icepick delivers a message to bring in a bag of marijuana or a pint of scotch or he is going tell of both incidents and he has hidden the stationary as proof of contraband brought into the Pen by the officer. The next day Icepick alerts the captain that the new officer is bringing in contraband drugs or alcohol, and the new officer is arrested bringing it in by the FBI who reads him his rights, As a result of being played by the inmate the officer is convicted and sentenced to 18 months in federal custody. His wife divorces him.

This is tragic, but it could all have been averted by taking care of business and following policy. An inmate's wife dying?—by policy an officer should refer death notification activity to the chaplain. The new officer gives the inmate a pass to the chapel after calling the chaplain and making sure one is in the office. The inmate goes to the chaplain's office and the chaplain calls the case manager to get the wife's name on the visitor's list. Turns out the inmate is not even married. The chaplain has the choice now to write a shot for the inmate lying to a staff member. The inmate loses for playing his game of deception and the new officer keeps his job. If you fall for the game and give an inmate any item of value, he can try to play you. DON'T DO IT! DO NO PERSONAL FAVORS.

I talk about the "nothing in and the nothing out" rule. Even a stick of gum can be wetted and used to imprint a key on a key ring while staff is distracted. Gum is just as malleable as putty and can be used for a face color on an object to look like a face sleeping in bed. You can gum up a lock. If you come inside the Pen and chew gum and throw it away, the inmate can dig it out of trash. An inmate will ask to borrow your metal government pen and "forget" to give it back. The ink can be used for tattoos and the pen can be sharpened into a shank. If you take nothing into the prison and take nothing out of the prison, including coded messages to inmate families, you can keep your good government job and maybe retire in 20 years, assuming you do a good job.

Many an officer came up to me after that I & F training story and told me something like this, "Chap, you saved my job! It wasn't a day, or a week, later that an inmate asked me for money, my pen, to make a call home for him, or to do a favor for him, and all I could think about was that story and "nothing in and nothing out" and "no favors rule." Thanks a lot."

Also, your personal information is a valuable commodity in prison. Your pictures on your desk of your wife and children tell an inmate you are married with kids. They can use that as a wedge. Your personal medical information is private. If you tell a staff member in front of an inmate you are going to the doctor for arthritis in your knee, you may as well have announced it on the inmate loud speaker. I never mentioned I was married or what part of town I lived in, and my phone was unlisted. No medical issues were ever disclosed.

I finally got to go to Basic Training at FLETC in Glynco, Georgia after each chaplain had taken much of their well-earned annual leave and I filled in for them. I was 42 and worried about being as fit as others because we had to run and lift weights, but I did all right. I lucked out and got paired with a 6-foot-4 ex-tackle from Lewisburg who was 24 and wanted to be an officer. He was my self-defense partner. He was gentle and easy with the old man and liked "the chap." The women in the class could tear wrists up and threw you down so hard it took your breath away. I passed the written test, the self-defense test, and the weapons test. Turns out that, as a chaplain, I was not supposed to fire a weapon, but no one told me that, so I qualified before they found or discovered that I should not have been firing on the range with the other staff. When they discovered this, the staff got a kick out of the fact that the chap was a shooter, and they put my grouping of bullet holes up in my room at night and placed the wording, "Rev. Rambo" above the grouping. The nickname stuck, but I did not object because my scores on tests gave me honor grad status and a $500 check. At that time, unless you fired a weapon and got over 95% on self-defense, weapons score and test score you could not be in the running for honor grad. Not bad for an old 42-year-old man.

The real risk is that if you fail on tests at FLETC, you do not go back to work. You are out of a job. For a person with career conditional status in the government, I was risking a lot by being a chaplain, which is an excepted appointment in Civil Service, and the Warden can fire you at any time for cause. There is a risk of failure on a test, but if you even study or listen at all, I believe most people will do well enough to pass. Here is a tip—don't drink alcohol during the day or drink too much at night in a bar and get into a fight at FLETC. You will be fired, as some of my class discovered.

Rev. Rambo came back all trained and rearing to go. I checked in at the Keyroom with a metal chit, got my keys and went to the work detail assigned to me. I checked off all the inmate names I had in my area, and if they were not there, I started looking for them in the Unit. If they were more than an hour late with no prior excuse (like going to the doctor or having a visit that I could verify), then I called them in as absent. It helps to prevent escape attempts. I assigned all the inmates duties, like cleaning the chapel floor and room, cataloguing books, typing the church bulletin on the typewriter.

As Volunteer Coordinator for the Pen I evaluated all 22 volunteer programs and did what was needed. I evaluated the Native American Sweat Lodge needs at the Pen and Camp, and met them as required. I did my safety reports and tracked all my cleaning chemicals on MSDS sheets. I looked at volunteer badges and updated them. I did my reports to the chaplains and to the Associate Warden and Camp Administrator. I worked my two days at the Atlanta Penitentiary and three days at the Federal Prison Camp. I made rounds at the Detention Center units on all three floors, and visited Segregation once a week. I preached at the Camp every Sunday and took turns preaching inside the Pen. There were five chaplains after a few years and the job got a bit easier than when we were only three chaplains for service to almost 2750 inmates (1500 Pen, 750 Detention Center Unit, 500 Camp).

I did the best I could to recruit, train and supervise volunteers on a part-time basis, but after I left they hired a full-time Volunteer Coordinator. I loved that job and met some of the finest people as volunteers I have ever known. Jack Hamilton and Doile King came more than 30 years inside the Pen. Dr. Meinert Grumm and his wife were in their 70s teaching Bible study in the Camp every Thursday night. Lorenzo Wright of Prison Fellowship taught Bible Study every Tuesday night in the Camp for more than 25 years. Ruby Pugh and Abundant Life church came for 15 years or more. Gordon Wadsworth, 30 years, Sam McGee and Al Stanley of Crusade for Christ came for years and years too many to mention. Gordon and Lorenzo are still coming there as I write this book.

Two volunteers, Tom Bluewolf and Winterhawk, helped the Native American inmates in their spiritual struggles. Lenny Habif was a great Jewish volunteer and Michael "Mickey" Elliston was a great Buddhist teacher in the Pen. Imam Furquan Muhammad was a great teacher of Sunni Muslims in the Camp and Pen. I hope they do not mind my mentioning them by name, but I do so because I honor them and respect them as heroes in the truest sense of the word. They gave their time voluntarily to help inmates be better persons. They each walked the talk of their faith.

In some ways the volunteers made more of a difference than we did or we could do as staff. Inmates did not really trust us as we carried keys and had control over them. I was called a "hack in the black," and "a man of the BOP not GOD," and other names unmentionable. The Camp Administrator's secretary said when I was conducting parole hearings I was known as "Throw the book Cook," and now I should be known as "Read the good book Cook." I was not liked by inmates because I was so "by the book," but I was respected. The inmates did not have the same axes to grind against the volunteers, and the volunteers were viewed as inmate helpers. In nine years we only had to terminate two volunteers. The inmates responded well to the volunteers' programs, and the volunteers did a lot to keep the tension of the place down.

In federal prison there are many diverse religions, and you are the chaplain who will be expected to have extensive and detailed knowledge of each or to request assistance from the regional or central office chaplain if you do not. To name a few, we had Protestant, Mormon, Roman Catholic, Buddhist, Hindu, Seventh Day Adventist, Jehovah Witness, Jewish, Muslim (Sunni, Shiite, Sikh, Nation of Islam, Moorish Science Temple of America) Rastafarian, Santeria, Native American, and even some Wiccan and Druid sects.

As a chaplain and also to maintain security, I was expected to show religious respect and tolerance for all forms of religious expression. I never approved a religion called Odinism and one called Creationism that was a front for Aryan Brotherhood. I did not approve a request by a sect of Santeria that wanted to cut pigeon heads off and have a key (prohibited object) and a throwing star (a weapon) sent in as a religious artifact. The way I rejected the Camp inmate's request for a key and a star was to fully research the rare sect of Santeria, called Yoruba, which he represented. He maxed out a short sentence before I got all the answers. Other inmates told me he planned to sue me as soon as I officially rejected his request. I never did reject it officially. I continued to research the request and even asked for a legal opinion and regional help right up to his release.

I once had a witch, or warlock, come into the chapel wanting to make a "pastoral call" to his witch's *koven* in Atlanta. He was a Canadian inmate and a psychological referral case out of Butner, and I would not permit the phone call because he had no organized religion to claim. But he found a witch's koven address in Atlanta and he wrote them. They wrote him back and said they did not understand his letters or his symbols, and they rejected him as a witch. I told a colleague it is a sad day when you get rejected from a witch's koven. I am not sure there is anything lower than that.

A U.S. District Judge, Edward Nottingham, once ordered the Warden at FCI Englewood to allow a Church of Satan adherent to perform rituals in the chapel (civil case 92-N-1515, dated October 7, 1994). If ordered, I would have refused to do this and either been fired, transferred or they would have worked around me to comply with the court order. There are certain ecclesiastical violations I cannot live with and this is one. A statement in the court order concerns me when it says "We should not lightly conclude that because of its content, Satanism is to be denied the full protection of the first amendment... We ought to give the Devil his due." Not this chaplain. I would quit first and am glad I never encountered this.

As a federal prison chaplain, you are expected to observe Ramadan and Jewish Passover and holidays, Jehovah Witness communion with a special wine, Christmas, Easter, Native American Solstice events, Powwows or Sweat lodges, and you are responsible for placing inmates on religious callouts for religious events. For example, every Friday afternoon we had to list about 75 inmates on Juma meeting for a Nation of Islam meeting and they would view Farrakhan videos or speeches. So all 75 would come in and give you their pass from their work detail to attend Juma Meeting, and when they left the meeting they would ask their pass to be signed by you. We had about 150 Sunni Muslims on callouts for Juma Prayer on Friday afternoon as well with the same pass requirements. So a chaplain worked the Pen on Fridays and he could be responsible for as many as 225 inmates in the chapel area to attend Juma meeting or prayer.

Every Saturday the Native Americans went into a hot sweat lodge in the Pen and at the Camp, so the chaplains had to make sure they had firewood and rocks to be heated. We usually had about 10 to 12 at both places, but the difficulty was to supply firewood and rock every week. Some chaplains had to purchase it, but we used camp inmates to cut the trees and split them into logs. That required supervision of the inmates with the axes to do the cutting and either a chaplain or a maintenance crew staff worker had to supervise.

I recruited a Spiritual Leader from the Star Clan of the Muscogee tribe and a peacekeeper from the Cherokee tribe to assist us in these efforts and it really cut down on the administrative remedies and lawsuits from Native Americans. I never sweated with the inmates in the lodge, but when the spiritual leader came in I did smoke the peace pipe in a healing ceremony and stood in a circle with him and the inmates.

A volunteer was the spiritual leader of the inmates. His name was Bluewolf and he taught me about Native American spirituality.

I greatly respect him. He taught me to respect Mother Earth or she will die and then she will not reproduce anything. He taught me to respect Grandfather Rock because he was here long before us and will be here long after us someday our dust will return to Grandfather Rock If we remember this, we will not get too full of ourselves. He taught me the Talking Stick way of handling problems, and I used that many times in my ministry later on. The inmates all sat in a circle and passed the talking stick and he used a hawk feather at the end of stick that resembled a small totem pole. When you had the Stick you talked as long as you wanted and everyone just deeply listened to you. Then when you were finished you passed the Stick to the next person to talk as long as they wanted. No questions or interruptions were allowed.

When Native American inmates had problems in the Pen or the Camp the spiritual leader would come in and pass the Talking Stick around and the problems got solved. I heard from inmates that fights and murders were avoided by talking out some of the tensions with the Talking Stick.

Native Americans had religious and constitutional rights and rights under special treaties when in federal custody. The Native American inmates had the right to worship their religion when incarcerated, as all inmates did. I once got sued by a Native American inmate because I went to the Lieutenant over Segregation about a request by the inmate to smoke a peace pipe. The Native American inmate who was sentenced for child molestation had been locked up in Seg for fighting. While there he requested a peace pipe to smoke. We talked about it in the chapel and all chaplains thought it was okay, but the Lieutenant checked with the captain who said there was a no smoking policy in Seg. The captain wanted it strictly enforced with no exceptions. I said okay and left, and the next week I got word that the inmate was suing the captain and me for violating his religious rights. The Legal Services unit of the penitentiary and the U.S. Attorney's Office represented us, and the case was dismissed.

Four incidents were very unsettling to me, but that just comes with being a chaplain. On one occasion a Rastafarian 6-foot-4 guy came into the chaplain's office at the Pen one night when I was working there alone (back when we did not have enough radios to go around). This guy had killed two people for some organized group of drug dealers. The group killed people with a shower of bullets to keep drug users who scammed them in line. This guy's girlfriend had sent him a package that said 'religious material' on it. It was a Rasta crown cap, and tucked in it was some black shiny female hosiery, which was obviously not religious and was contraband, so it was going to be sent back to the woman who sent it. When he came to the chapel I had to tell him, we could not give him the hosiery. He talked to me in very loud agitated tones getting louder each time he spoke. He demanded I give him what was sent to him. Every time he would get louder I would wait about two seconds, pause, look at him square in the eyes and say the same thing, "I am sorry I cannot give you hosiery, as it is contraband." I can only guess why he wanted hosiery. When he left he slammed the door so hard the glass shook and, I thought for sure he had cracked something, but he didn't. I used this "slow down and talk calm" approach on several occasions. It always worked for me because if you get louder because he gets louder it goes up a notch at a time until you are screaming at each other in an intense manner This is what he wants so he can justify doing violence against you.. If you don't give him much, he can't react that much or that loudly for long.

The next day I went to the captain and begged for a radio in the chapel when working alone. I got radios for the chapel authorized two years later after the institution had a murder of a staff member by an inmate. That murder of a staff member was the toughest incident I have ever had to handle.

I took that murder hard and did not do well in coping with it. It was in late December 1993, and it involved an inmate who was in for murder. He borrowed a hammer from another inmate on the plumbing detail, walked around behind the officer and hit him in the back of the head near the brain stem several times. I was the only chaplain on duty that Wednesday morning, and I went with the Associate Warden to Grady Hospital. By then the officer's head had swollen from the blood and he was almost unrecognizable. I prayed for him and his family. I found his mother and father in South Carolina and they came that night to the hospital. The officer died the next morning at eight a.m. I assisted in the funeral in South Carolina and Attorney General Reno presented the family with a flag.

The reason I took it so hard was because my own step-brother was beaten to death in 1977 by two men and I relived a bit of that again during this murder of a very likeable officer in the Pen. I did not know the officer well, but I worked on weights with him at the outside gym and I had talked about football with him on several occasions. His name was Tony Washington and I listed his name to honor him on a memorial every April during National Crime Victims' Rights Week for the next 15 years.

After that murder I changed. I still had six years to go to retire, but inmates got a very different chaplain in me after that murder. I was 100% professional with inmates at all times and fair but firm, and actually not friendly at all. I took care of business but did not get involved in small talk or spend any more time than I had to. It did not help that after the lockdown because of the murder of an officer, the inmates were strolling the halls, and would whistle, "If I had a hammer I would hammer in the morning...."

All staff at the Pen were debriefed after the murder through the help of outside professionals, but I went to an outside counselor for myself on four occasions because I needed help. I was so angry at times I felt like I was seething inside. The inmate was moved to nearby FCI Talladega where he broke the back of a friend of mine during a forced cell move attempt. A forced cell move is when six guys each dressed like Darth Vader go into the cell, which the inmate often smeared with baby oil or feces and each officer takes a body part, such as a leg or an arm or a head, and physically removes the inmate from his cell to another more secure cell, which sometimes involves tied restraints. The friend, who was a case manager, was filling in for officers for the forced cell move and the inmate pushed off a wall and pushed my friend against the side of a toilet bowl and broke his back. He was partially paralyzed and had to retire early on disability. The mayhem this one inmate caused is enormous. The reason the inmate was incarcerated was that he killed a woman on federal property. He later killed an officer at the Pen with a hammer, and then broke the back of a case manager at Talladega. I still to this day have unresolved anger feelings toward that inmate, and I am glad I am not his chaplain. I try to give the feelings to God and lay them down at the foot of the cross, but I keep picking them back up again for some reason. I have some investment in staying mad at that inmate. Maybe someday I will lay it down and not pick it back up with God's help and grace.

The third incident happened with a Nation of Islam inmate who was a drug enforcer that killed several people in the southern states. He had a gold tooth which glistened when he smiled. One day I told him he could not store personal items in the religious locker in the Pen. He ran up to me in the hallway right before Juma Meeting on Friday afternoon and was screaming at me that I was a racist and had a problem with him every time I came in from the Camp and what a sorry excuse for a person I was. He then got about six inches from my face and was spewing saliva as he spoke loudly, so the other 74 inmates in the Juma Meeting could hear as well, "Do you have a problem with me?" I waited about three seconds as I saw the blood in his eye and said calmly but firmly and without backing up an inch but putting my left front foot in front to brace for a battle or a quick hit, and I said, "I do not have a problem with you. Do you have a problem with me?" There was a pause of about 10 seconds, maybe even 20, as we looked at each other and he sized me up. I could not help but wonder if he thought he could take me. I gave him nothing. I sort of Zenned out. I did not back up, did not lift my hand to remove the saliva on my face, and was waiting for a quick move from him, and I was going to defend myself to the end. It never came. Thank God.

If something had developed, I was in the chapel by myself, again with no radio, with 75 Nation of Islam inmates and one of them was in my face big time, one who just happened to have murdered several people in his young life. His file said it took 20 armed SWAT officers to surround him and arrest him. Here I was, one lone chaplain facing him off by myself with no radio for assistance. Sometimes all you have is your personal integrity and your own strength of self in those moments. Choose wrong and you are dead. Choose right and you live. I was not going to back up to him or show fear. Never, ever! Not to any inmate I ever met. Of course, I was afraid in that moment but I was not going to show it.

I decided to not write that Nation of Islam inmate up for misconduct (spewing saliva on my face, for one thing, could be grounds). He did yell, but he did not make an overt threat. I was not afraid to write him up, but apparently he had gotten a *Dear John* letter earlier and had bad news from home. I decided to let it pass. That is what I mean by occasionally showing grace.

The fourth incident involved an Islamic inmate at the camp. The Federal Prison Camp in Atlanta holds 500 minimum security inmates, and there were many drug offenders, short-time offenders and some white collar offenders. Occasionally, the Camp received some hard-time offenders nearing release from the Pen. That was the case with Rasheed (not his real name). Rasheed was sentenced for bank robbery/parole violation for 12 years and was near his release date, and the Pen transferred him to the Camp. Rasheed was a federal parole violator as he was serving a federal sentence for bank robbery and released on parole when he acted as a getaway car driver for another bank robbery. He also attacked his girlfriend with a knife while on parole but did not hurt her, and no charges were filed. When arrested for the bank robbery, he had a small amount of cocaine with him (he received two years in Georgia to run concurrently for the small amount of cocaine). He was on parole and given five years as a parole violator. His five year parole violator term ran concurrently with all other sentences. This kind of criminal background demonstrates that this is not a naïve inmate; he was street smart and savvy to jail life. When he arrived at the Camp, he came into my office and tried to convert me to Islam. He told me Jesus Christ is a fairytale, like Santa Claus, and all who believe in the fairytale are going to Hell.

I did not respond to Rasheed's shock techniques. I asked him what he was in for and he said he is incarcerated for parole technical violations like failing to report. I asked him if he was sure about that and he said yes. I asked how his faith resolves or forgives a liar and he said it does not accept a liar. I said you lied to me twice. He said he has not lied to me, and took offense at my calling him a liar. I said now that is three times you have lied to me. The first was when you said you were a technical violator. The second was when you confirmed that lie. The third was when you said you did not lie and resented being called a liar. You were on parole for a bank robbery conviction when you drove a car in a bank robbery and you are here as a parole violator for new criminal offenses including bank robbery, cocaine possession and attacking a woman with a knife. You are not here for merely a technical violation. You tried to game the wrong chaplain. I have read your file. You need to ask Allah to forgive you for lying to me and to ask me to forgive you as well. He looked at me for a long time and without saying a word got up and left my office. I knew he did not fit into the Camp. He was too street smart for these Camp inmates.

Soon after Rahseed's arrival he took over the Islamic group of inmates and selected the biggest, meanest guy in the camp to walk around with him all the time. I will call this guy Foreman (George Foreman was his hero). Rahseed had a routine set of techniques he used to win converts to Islam. He was Sunni Muslim and he would walk up to Christians in the dorm and tell them Jesus Christ was a fairytale and everyone who believed in that fairytale was going straight to Hell. He would then ask if their mother or grandmother was a Christian and most people would say yes. Then he would say "your grandmother is in hell then and I sure hope you don't go there." That would cause a huge emotional reaction and then they were off on a heated argument, which is what he wanted all along because this is his personal holy jihad to convert Christians to Islam. The argument would have led to a fist fight if Foreman had not been looming behind all the time. Rasheed also made sure each inmate was alone when he went through his routine, so it always made it two to one if there was a fight.

Rahseed said that Allah cannot beget himself, therefore Jesus cannot be the Son of God and it is an unpardonable sin (shirk) if you believed that kind of fairytale. The tension level in the Camp rose like crazy after Rasheed came there and spouted his religious propaganda. Two inmates, one an associate member of organized crime in South Carolina and the other a drug enforcer for a drug group in North Carolina came to my office. They said, "Chaplain, we need your help. Rasheed is saying things like my grandmother is in Hell. We are thinking about taking this matter into our own hands. What is your advice since this is really a religious matter almost like a religious war?" I replied, "If you two are telling me you are going to assault Rasheed or kill him, I will have to report this and have you both locked up. Is that what you are saying, or are you saying you just want some advice?" One inmate said, "No, we are not saying that we are going to harm him—we just want to know your ideas."

I was silent and thinking for about two minutes. I said the next time Rasheed says his routine I want you to walk up to him and get close to him and look him in the eye and say, "Rasheed, I got one thing I want to say to you: I am a wall." Say or do nothing else and just stand there. The inmate replied, "Chaplain, that is the craziest thing I have ever heard. That does not even make sense. We don't understand you." I said, "Just do it. You asked for my advice and you know I have been around the block a while. Just do it and see what happens."

The two inmates complied. When Rasheed started in on them, they would stand near him and say "I am a wall." Rasheed would flounder around and bluster at them and say, "What do you mean you are a wall? I don't understand that. Foreman, what the heck is he talking about—I am a wall? That does not make any sense." On and on he would fluster and bluster. But no other reaction or words would come out from the attacked inmate. Soon, everyone in the dorm caught on and would say to Rasheed after his religious verbiage "Rasheed, I am a wall, too." Then other dorms heard and they would do the same, and no matter where Rasheed went in the Camp to spout his verbiage he got, "I am a wall, too."

Rasheed was not a happy camper. He went to the Camp Administrator and asked to be transferred back to the Penitentiary. The Camp Administrator told him, "No, Rasheed, this is not a hotel and I would think you would not want to go behind the Wall again. Transfer denied." Camp inmates referred to the Pen as "going behind the Wall." Rasheed served his time and was marginalized and no one got hurt or killed. The Camp went back to being a regular Camp, tensions lessened, and Foreman stopped hanging around Rasheed. Rasheed lost his power and influence. The day he was released from the Camp and his cab came to pick him up, I was standing near Release and Discharge. Right before he got into the cab I wished him well and said that I wanted him to know something. He replied,

"What is that, Chaplain?" I said, "I wish you well. I am a wall, too." He looked at me, squinted, and said, "It was you all along, wasn't it? You were behind it." I said, "Yep. It sure was. You should not have lied to me."

Sometimes things like "I am a wall" just come to you from the outside as if from a divine source. It allowed the one being attacked to state his position in a strong way without being aggressive or inviting a hostile comeback. It said that "I am unmoved as a wall is" in my Christian faith by your attacks or your jihad against my faith and beliefs if you will. I also thought about saying, "I am a well," into which you can put your verbiage and it will go to the bottom, but it would not have had the same effect as "I am a wall." If the situation reversed and a Muslim inmate came to me and said another inmate was threatening him to believe in Jesus Christ and insulting his relatives, I would say, "Be a wall."

One of the things you often run across in prison is inmates with medical problems. About 10-15% in the Pen had AIDS or Hepatitis B, which is highly contagious. The same advice to staff about not disclosing your medical condition to inmates I would give to inmates. Once everyone knows you have a serious contagious disease they will not associate with you or want to work with you on an inmate work detail. I was asked to take an inmate with Hepatitis B on my chapel detail at the Camp. I did so and I was glad I did. This inmate was so thankful someone would let him work for them that he worked very hard and was honest and I could count on him to do a task from start to finish in a quality way. He worked for me about a year. He accepted Christ and appeared to be genuine about his faith and his walk. He once had a paper cut and was typing on the electronic typewriter and I asked him to go to medical and get it cared for and to take the rest of the day off. I spent the rest of the day cleaning and re-cleaning the typewriter keys. I risked my own safety and the safety of my inmate crew, but we tried to be smart about it and never allow any blood to be present from the infected inmate. It is a little like how Jesus must have felt when he worked with lepers. People with Hepatitis and AIDS are children of God just like the rest of us.

One inmate at the Pen had full-blown Aids and wanted to have a prayer rug in the Visiting Room and pray with his wife. One of the other chaplains denied the request as it was against policy and the inmate threatened to "beat his bald head bloody." When he first made the request, he spewed saliva in the face of the other chaplain, and the chaplain had to be tested for AIDS. The inmate was quickly transferred.

That is why I think it is important to read the inmate's file. You get a heads up by knowing the inmate is capable of violence or has serious mental or medical problems. Case managers have the complete file in their unit or in a central area, and occasionally I would go pull several files of inmates and just read for a few hours.

After reading the file on one inmate who wanted to work on my chapel detail in the Pen, I said, no. I did not want him to work there. I told the other chaplains the inmate would be a risk to us because he manipulates the phone call privileges to make illegal calls, like to his lawyer when he says he is calling his rabbi. The inmate was Jewish and was already trying to manipulate his way into the detail for his own ends. I went on vacation and the inmate was assigned to our detail by the other chaplain in direct contradiction to my wishes. When I got back, the inmate was on the detail. I saw him and fired him within five minutes, which is how long it took me to call the inmate into my office and tell him to go back to his unit to be re-assigned. The other chaplain and I had a frank discussion. Soon thereafter, it came out that the inmate was calling his girlfriend from the chapel when I was away, and alleging it was a religious call. The girlfriend was alleging to the institution that she was an attorney, which she was not. This allowed her to see him more often for attorney-client meetings but she was not a real attorney. The inmate stole an expensive watch from her while in the visiting room and it was a real mess. By the way, part of the reason the inmate was transferred to the Atlanta Pen was he was using the chapel phone to make illegal calls and the chaplains at his previous institution had gotten into trouble for letting him.

This raises an important issue of what you can do to be fired or reprimanded as a chaplain in a prison. Don't give poor inmates tennis shoes or clothing you bring in for them; don't bring anything in like a video sent from a family member and mailed to your home that has cocaine hidden in the video; don't accept a Bible with dollar bills sewn into the cover; don't let an inmate make a phone call to a terrorist, a lawyer or a judge; don't have sex with an inmate or watch him have sex with himself in the chaplain's office; don't lie to a supervisor when questioned; don't accept money or a job or a business deal with an inmate or a member of an inmate's family; don't have a stock-advising inmate tell you what stocks to buy; don't cover for an inmate who did something wrong in your chapel—like hiding contraband there; don't go to the hospital to administer last rites to a dying inmate and curse out the nursing staff and give short shrift to the inmate's dying request; don't write love letters on your office computer to a former female inmate you worked within a state prison chaplain's job; don't visit pornographic sites on your office computer; don't bring a cell phone into the prison; don't push or slap an inmate first; don't ask for a computer to be sent to your home from an inmate's wife; don't take a prison file home; don't allow an inmate to be on your office computer or to fix your computer; don't let an inmate have a key to anything including his own desk he uses when typing for you; don't let an inmate on your detail fail to report to your work and you just let it slide and it turns out he is trying to escape; don't fail to secure your keys and lose them; don't give a death message (of a family member who died) to the wrong inmate or fail to check out the accuracy of the death message first; don't let an inmate hear personal information such as your credit card number when purchasing travel over the phone, or a serious problem you are having in your family, or a medical condition you have—everything I just mentioned happened to a chaplain I either knew or heard of while I worked in federal prison. I could call state and federal prison chaplains central offices and ask them to list about a thousand other don'ts for prison chaplains, but the bottom line is to forbid an inmate to jeopardize the order or security of the institution you work in. Often that requires common sense and listening to that little voice in your conscience that whispers, "Don't do this—it is wrong,"

Being a prison or jail chaplain is a work of God. It is not taking Jesus Christ into the prison as many think because Christ is already there. It is connecting Christ to the right inmate at the right time.

Some inmates are tired of prison life and crime, and hungry for the Word, and when they hear it or see it they soak it up. In nine years I think I preached over 500 sermons, delivered more than 700 death messages (about 85 a year), arranged the marriage for about 20 inmates with outside clergy, visited thousands in administrative segregation, suicide watch detail, max Seg, hospital, and during lockdowns. I baptized about 10 a year. I prayed with and counseled many an inmate in my office. I used the Sinners Prayer when an inmate was breaking down and asking for help to find God or know Christ. I ran 22 volunteer programs as the Volunteer Coordinator for about 21 different faith groups. I tried to be a chaplain to all faiths or those of no faith and even to those who lied to or stole from me.

Remember that *Scofield Reference Bible* I threw at an inmate in the county jail in 1970? Well that Bible was given to me by my sister in 1960 and she died of diabetes in 1983. I only have a few pictures of my sister and that Bible was a keepsake. She gave it to me when I was about 14 years old. She had written a personal inscription to me inside the cover. She was a wonderful believer, and her words were encouraging to me. I had carried that Bible for over 30 years when an inmate in the Prison Camp stole it from me. I had left it out after a sermon on the pulpit, and when I came back from the Visiting Room it was gone. I brooded about it and at first was very mad. Then a revelation hit me. Maybe the thief would read that very Bible and he would convert to Christianity. I knew every word by heart of what my sister wrote, so I went out and bought another *Scofield* just like the stolen one and inscribed the exact words in it all over again. No one can steal the Word from me because it is in my mind and my heart as was my sister's words, which guided me for many years even after she was gone.

I heard that Vietnam POWs created a Bible from memory because their captors would not let them have a Bible. They each pieced together what they could remember, wrote that part down and passed it around to one another. I forgave the thief and prayed that he might accept Christ by reading that very same stolen Bible. He could not steal what was Eternal Writ. All my anger and brooding went away.

The one thing that stands out more than anything in chaplain prison work is communion. Communion and offering Jesus Christ to inmates during the communion service was a special time and an honor and a privilege for me. It is a sacred event and the Holy Spirit of Jesus Christ guides and directs it and infuses it in such a way that the power of it swept over me and everyone participating in it in prison. Maybe it is because in prison there is so much anguish and suffering going on, maybe in prison there is a feeling of guilt that needs to be assuaged and forgiven, maybe it is the feeling of communion itself that swept over us all in that Christ gave up his body and Spirit for even me as wretched as I am. But when an inmate asked me before I retired what was the best thing I did as chaplain, without hesitation I said "Communion."

Communion made everything right again. Maybe the inmate had just received a Jody letter from his wife that she was divorcing him for a Jody. Maybe his appeal was denied. Maybe he just got a misconduct report for some stupid thing he did. Maybe his kids were in trouble with the law or a relative just died and he cannot go to the funeral. Maybe the family is losing the house because he cannot pay the bills. Then he takes communion with the wafer and the grape juice representing the body and blood of Jesus Christ. He feels saved from his life of sin and death and from all his woes and troubles, and he feels so humble and grateful that Jesus died for even him who is so unworthy that he feels overwhelmed by that selfless love. I am personally very, very grateful that I was fortunate enough to witness inmates and myself (and the families could come too at the Camp setting only) taking communion together. They heard me preach Christ. The inmate choir sang about Christ. Inmate readers read about and studied Christ in Chapel and Bible study, but when we ingested the symbols of Christ—something mystical happened that rose above all other things. No matter how many wrongs we had done in this life we were all made right in communion if we sincerely asked for forgiveness and took the sacred elements.

One funny thing happened when I had an intern from Candler Theological Seminary come to be trained as a prison chaplain. The intern wanted to do an early Easter Sunday event outside at the prison Camp. I allowed him to plan the service and to conduct it, but I warned him to keep the top on the wafers when serving communion or they might blow away in the wind. Well he forgot and opened the top and suddenly a gust of strong wind hit the tray and about 100 wafers blew away on the ground. He was so embarrassed and scared I thought he was going to have a heart attack on the spot. I told him, "My friend you have now been disaster-proofed as a prison chaplain for nothing quite like that will ever happen to you again and now you will always remember to cover the wafer tray when serving communion outside."

Also, I supervised many Salvation Army interns and I did not know the Salvation Army does not take communion because their founder, William Booth, felt every meal should be a communion with the Lord and not just at communion table. I was embarrassed when I asked them to do a service for me when we were serving communion and none of them partook of the wafers or grape juice. When I learned what was going on, I always scheduled them for a non-communion Sunday after that.

The Salvation Army prison volunteers were a great group. They donated Bibles and Christmas cards and provided about five Sundays a year of interns who conducted much of the service. They provided a nice break from my own preaching, and the interns played music that was quite good. But that brings me to the inmate choir. I usually had about 25 men who could sing and play music like I have never heard even to this day. They would practice during the week and sing on Sundays and at special events like a thanksgiving and Christmas concert.

Once, we had Babbie Mason come in, and she sang "Holy Spirit Come Down," with our choir playing the background music and singing accompaniment to her. She may have been just being nice but later remarked, "That choir could go with me on the road they were so good." The choir was one thing the men could do pretty much on their own, and they took great pride in singing for their families who came to church on Sunday with them. It was different inside the Pen because no families could come to the chapel service, but inmate choirs in the Pen were quite good as well. In fact, it seems a barometer of health for the prison chapel as to how well the choir does. If the inmate choir is outstanding and sings their heart out every Sunday there seems to be energy around the chapel that is positive. When the choir is at each other's throats or jealousies emerge as to who gets to solo the most, there is a negative spirit around the chapel as well.

Wardens and supervisors judged me by how clean I keep my chapel area. They figure if the chapel is not clean I cannot control and supervise the inmates who work on my detail. Our prison chapel was spotless and I always made sure I had a buffer that worked and plenty of wax even if I had to finagle a buffer or two from some other detail. The chapel was never dirty. I kept a white cloth that I would rub over things and if it came back with dirt on it, we cleaned it again.

I always knew where every inmate was on my detail. If he left a note that he was going to the doctor, I called to make sure he was at the doctor's office or in his cube or cell as a sick inmate. If he did not show up on my detail within an hour and, he had not told me or anyone else on the work detail about a visit or sick call and I could not locate him in the unit or hospital, I called the Lieutenant to see if he could find him and if we could not, we issued an incident report for failing to report to the work detail. The reason I did this was to maintain good order and security because the inmates would get lazy or lie in their bed if they thought they could get by with it. They would on rare occasion be trying to escape and I did not want to be asleep on my watch when they tried. Also, you can be fired or reprimanded for not supervising your work crew when one tries to escape and you did not notice he was gone.

Again I mention that inmates did not like me but they did respect me. By the Book Cook did want them to toe the line, but I was also there to counsel and pray for them and they knew that too. Chaplains and psychologists are usually thought of as the good guys in prison, and you really have to work hard to be thought of as a bad guy. I was never fully trusted by inmates because I carried keys and they knew I would lock them up in Seg if they crossed the line with me. Consequently, I rarely had to take action against inmates for misconduct. I was clear with them from the start on this point. I think lack of clarity leads to problems in prison.

I am not sure you can teach street savvy in seminary to prepare a chaplain for the prison environment unless you encourage a prospective chaplain to use his or her field training or practicum in a prison setting, such that a veteran prison chaplain can train the new chaplain in the ways and wiles of prison life. When I started in a county jail there was no training at all, and I was thrust into a prison life that I neither understood nor knew how to cope with. The federal prison model is much better than that, and you go to training very soon after being hired and then go to in-service training for 40 hours every year as a refresher.

The most important lesson I learned from the training was that every employee was a security person first and foremost and second he was a chaplain or psychologist or doctor or whatever position he or she held. I never forgot that lesson, and if chaplains disagree with that training and think they are chaplains first and foremost and secondarily they are security officers, they will be in for a long, tough ride at their institutions they serve. Seminary leads one to conclude that we are here to serve God first and foremost. We should be loving, caring, comforting pastoral counselors and preachers, and we should help the oppressed. What seminary cannot teach you is a form of tough love that says you can be all that but first and foremost you are a security officer when you work in a prison.

As Volunteer Coordinator I had to run criminal background checks on prospective volunteers, and I found a child molester, a rapist, a robber and a drug dealer who applied to be a volunteer and to come into our prison. I notified the volunteer we could not allow him or her in because of the criminal record. I found people lying about their former aliases and trying to cover a record by giving their present name only and not their former name, which would reveal the criminal record, I found a few Spanish-speaking volunteer applicants would give their name as something like Gonzales when their record was under Rodriguez –Gonzales and that way they tried to hide the record to gain entrance. I had to run Spanish names under Gonzales-Rodriguez, Rodriguez-Gonzales, Gonzales and Rodriguez to be sure there were no hits (criminal records) under all four possible names. I had to call three references and check on former employment and education, and if they lied on the applicant form, I would not admit them. I had to fingerprint them and send their prints into the FBI in Washington, DC. If the prints came back with a hit, they were terminated for not telling me. But first I notified them of the record and gave them a chance to dispute it. Occasionally there was an error in the record and they could volunteer after it was corrected.

I trained staff the same way I was trained. I emphasized that first and foremost we were all security personnel. I talked about respect and tolerance for other religions in prison. I explained the five pillars of Islam, the basics on Nation of Islam, the reason for Native Americans to have sweat lodges as required by treaties, rules, and rights of religious worship in prison as afforded by the Constitution. I explained the differences in Jehovah Witnesses, Seventh day Adventists, Jewish, Protestant, and Roman Catholics. I explained religious holidays and observances that would be honored by the inmate observing them if he wanted to be placed on callout that day to observe the religious holiday. I explained what went on at Ramadan for 30 days and the break the fast feast afterwards. I explained that certain religions were not as well known as others but that all valid religious groups would be honored and allowed. There would be other groups who were not yet considered valid religious groups like New Christian Identity and Creationism, but that they were always applying, and someday may be allowed but before that day they would not be allowed to meet and practice their religion in chapel.

I gave some examples that would help staff and volunteers understand. For example, a Native American wears a medicine bag that may contain a bone or a claw or a feather that is sacred to him. If an officer suspects the man of hiding contraband in the bag, he should *not* take the bag off the inmate, open it and finger all the elements inside. An officer once did this and the inmate kicked him in the side and broke three ribs. The inmate felt dishonored and disrespected. I talked to the inmate and he said, "Chaplain, how would you feel if you were taking communion and an officer stuck his finger in your cup and tasted it with his fingers because he suspected you were using real wine instead of grape juice? Would you be offended or upset? That is how I felt when he fingered my objects in my medicine bag." I always advised officers to ask the inmate to open his own medicine bag for visual inspection and to let the objects in the bag be taken out by the inmate and put back in by the inmate. Then there was no disrespect or dishonor involved.

A Rastafarian inmate wears dreadlocks and a headset called a Crown. Both have religious meaning to the Rastafarian. If an officer suspects drugs hidden in the hair or the crown, I advise the officer to ask the inmate to remove the Crown and show the headset inside and outside. If the officer suspects the hair to contain drugs, I advised the officer to make sure there is another officer present as witness and allow the inmate to move his hair around to see if drugs are hidden. If necessary and with another witness present, the officer has the right to move his fingers into the dreadlocks hair to ensure drugs are not being secreted.

Muslims and other followers of Islam have the religious right to wear a *kufi* and to order a prayer rug and other religious material to follow their religion in prison. They can request to be on a Friday callout from their work detail to attend Juma prayer. The Nation of Islam has the right to attend Juma Meeting on Friday and to request off their work detail and to be placed on callout from their work detail. It usually took two chaplains to supervise this labor intensive activity on Fridays. It really wore me out and I was very tired afterwards, especially when there were always a few inmates that were on the watch list and they had to be personally supervised so we knew every hour where they were by putting our eyes on them. If they were not locatable when they were supposed to be, we were supposed to notify the Lieutenant immediately.

We had the keys to all the combination locks and to all the locks in the chapel, and you almost get carpal tunnel just by opening all the locked doors and then locking them all after the inmates leave. I figure I opened and locked about a million doors in the nine years I was there, and I carried a wad of keys that weighed about a half a pound. The keys brushing against my pants leg wore out several pants near the pocket area.

The Native American Sweat Lodge was another labor intensive part of being a chaplain. We had one every Saturday at the Camp and every Saturday at the Pen. They had to build the lodge out of bent willows tied together resembling an igloo and use gray blankets covering the lodge to keep the heat inside the blankets. They used volcanic rocks or hard rocks to burn red hot over cut firewood. They would go into a quadrant of the sweat and they would open the door only occasionally to let the heat out. They believed they owned their sweat and their blood, and they would give this to the Creator during the sweat. They would sometimes confess to the Creator and ask for His understanding and forgiveness and for the Creator to grant his wisdom and guidance. Sometimes they smoked the peace pipe with *kinikinic* tobacco before the sweat. Sometimes they used the peace pipe or another object sacred to them as a talking stick and had a talking circle to talk out their problems.

One of my jobs was to make sure we had the firewood and the rocks every Saturday. Some chaplains purchase these things, but I got Camp inmates to split trees fallen around the grounds and use rocks from the grounds. Many a Thursday I went down to an area and got a Camp inmate to check out an axe and cut firewood. I even cut some myself. Keeping the Pen and Camp firewood stocked was labor intensive and many times I brought in the firewood from the Camp on a forklift to the Pen Sweat Lodge area. I think this fell under "other duties as assigned" somewhere in the fine print of my chaplain job description.

I made a good friend in this process because we needed a Native American volunteer for the inmates and did not have one. I looked in the yellow pages and called Native American Spirituality, and Tom Bluewolf answered the phone. He said I am at a creek come-together called Sautee Nacoochee, and I live there in a tipi. You can visit me there. It was an hour and a half drive from Atlanta and just North of Helen, GA. I told the Camp Administrator and the AW that I needed to go meet this guy because he would not come to the institution until he met me. They allowed me to go and I drove up to meet him

When I arrived on ceremonial Native American grounds, I saw his tipi at the foot of where the Sautee and Nacoocheee Rivers come together. He walked out of his tipi carrying a laptop. The old ways meet the new ways in Tom Bluewolf. He said little other than welcome and said he wanted to go sit in a medicine wheel area next to his tipi where two chairs were in a circle of rocks. We sat there for about 30 minutes and neither he nor I spoke. I was thinking out of respect for him I would not speak first and I was also enjoying the sun and getting out of the Pen. After 30 minutes of silence, he said, "I think you are a spiritual man. I will be your volunteer." He asked no questions. I gave him the application and I left.

Bluewolf brought so much spirituality into the Camp and the Pen that I had very few problems from about 10 Native American inmates at the Camp and about 15 at the Pen. He introduced the talking circle and used it at both places. He sweated with the inmates at both places. He resolved problems, and I would have not known about how he did it except one inmate at the Camp would come to my office and tell me that inmate so and so were going to have a fight, and Tom Bluewolf during the sweat said, "We are so few now, we do not need to fight and cause the Creator pain and lessen ourselves in the Creator's eyes." The fight never happened. Many conflicts were resolved in the talking circle and in the sweat by Bluewolf. But he was not a snitch. He never told me what he did. Other inmates told me and I was glad we had him as a volunteer. The year after I left the Pen made Bluewolf the Volunteer of the Year. I think of him as a good friend and have met him at World Expo events, Native American gatherings, and medicine councils at the Unitarian Church and at his home. He and Winterhawk, his friend and mine, will always have a position of respect in my eyes.

That brings me back to the volunteers and their years of service I cannot say enough about some of them serving over 30 years. There has to be a special place in God's kingdom for people who come to a federal prison weekly as a volunteer when it is raining or cold or they have the shingles or don't feel well and yet they hardly ever miss a week. They come to minister to the "least of these brethren" and they come in the name of God, Christ, Allah, Jehovah and the Creator.

I mother-henned my volunteers closely in order to ensure their protection from manipulation by the inmates and vice versa. I wrote about my volunteers in Volunteer Today to show my appreciation, and annually gave them a beautiful dinner and award night with certificates for every five years they completed. I often thanked them for coming and I took care of issues they raised. They did not understand the delays for getting their volunteer badge were because of an inmate disturbance that I could not reveal. I just used a code with them that the delay was unavoidable, and they understood. I could not tell them an inmate had escaped or been murdered or caused a forced cell change. They later found out anyway when the inmates told them. I have often wondered if I could have ever been a volunteer at a federal prison. I do not think I have it in me, and I am amazed, humbled and very grateful that they did. They truly did God's work and "visited those in prison."

As a prison chaplain, I had to work not only with volunteers but also with staff and inmates' family members. The way I worked with staff and inmates' families was very important. I encountered inmates' families in the visiting room, and when they called in to give a death message or extreme sickness or traffic accident in the family. I think the ministry of presence and listening and prayer helps the family when I hear their pain or sorrow and ask them if is all right to pray with them. I only had one person in all my years say that he preferred I did not pray with him as he said he was an atheist. I had a few inmates come back and tell me how grateful they were that I prayed with their moms when a mother would call to say her husband died and she wanted to inform her son in prison. I prayed sometimes with the mom on the phone and son listening in my office so the family could have a prayer together. I took down all the information and sent it to the case manager, but in the Pen they could not leave and go to the funeral. In the Camp they could request to go, but it was up to the Warden. Even when they were approved for a funeral furlough some inmates had to be escorted by staff. When the Warden decided not to let the Camp inmate go to the funeral, the inmate often wanted me to appeal the decision. I always felt the Warden knew a lot of information I did not know as staff listened in to inmate phone calls and the decision was beyond my pay grade. I did not appeal the Warden's decisions about funerals.

On two occasions throughout my career I did appeal the Warden's decision and that had to do with allowing dangerous volunteers with criminal records into the institution. He overruled me and allowed them both in and later regretted it, as one of the volunteers shot and killed a police officer a few years later and the other had a child molestation record 15 years earlier and appealed to the Warden to let him come in. The molester was later terminated for not showing up as expected or showing up 30 minutes before count time.

I knew the way I worked with all the associate warden's correctional officers, food staff, Inmate Systems, human resources, medical staff, psychologists, safety staff, and my own colleague chaplains could make me or break me. I did have one interesting discussion with a Warden over security about volunteers. I quoted a policy statement about not allowing volunteers in to the institution who had felony records, and the AW over security told me in front of the Warden that I was wrong. I explained I did not think I was wrong and maybe he had his facts confused. The Warden looked at me in mainline (when all of us stand during the noon meal) and said, "Chaplain are you willing to bet your career on what you just said." I looked at the Warden and AW and said, "I sure am. Will the AW bet his career on what he said?" (This conversation took place a long time after a previous Warden let the two volunteers with records come in to the institution, and I later learned we had to get regional office approval to allow a felon to come in. That is why I knew the policy so well) The Warden just looked at me for a moment and said, "The chaplain is probably right." Several days later the AW over security saw me in the rear corridor and said, "Chap, you were right about the policy." He just smiled at me.

I think it is important to know your policy, the rules for your chapel and volunteer area, and all other security rules inside and outside and if you are unclear or do not understand something clear it up because someday it could mean your job or maybe your life or someone else's if you break the policy. Take for instance the policy to secure my office. I have to go down the hall to the bathroom and because it is only my detail in the chapel I figure it is a few seconds, so I will leave my door open and unlocked. Inside is my computer and some sensitive files are on the computer. I am gone 90 seconds, and in that time Inmate Smith quietly opens my door and goes on my computer, looks up an inmate he suspects is cooperating, and finds out the inmate is an informant. My worker then takes some government pens he plans to sharpen as shanks. He uses the pen to kill the inmate that night. The investigation reveals he entered my office to get the information and the weapon. My dereliction of duty leads to an inmate murder. I ALWAYS locked my office door even when gone for a few seconds. I turned my computer off when I was leaving.

I repeat this because it is so important: Staff members need to trust me. They will observe me, and if I am as security-oriented as they are, they will see me as one of them. If not, they will watch me like an inmate.

Ministering to staff is not my primary job, but I felt it was important. I conducted the marriage for some officers and their spouses and did some funerals for officers and staff who died during their tenure. I counseled many a young officer as well as some staff who were having marital trouble, drinking problems, or gambling issues. I would venture to say that most officers had some marital trouble because the position of correctional officer carries so much stress on the job. All day long an officer deals with inmates who have been in trouble with authority all their lives. The daily doses of cortisol because of adrenaline surges from stress take their toll. At night the officer is drained and just wants to zone out in front of the TV or drink a pack of beers so he can get up and face the next day of 100 inmate demands and issues. Sometimes the shift rotates and an officer pulls night shifts for three months and just sleeps during the time his family is at home.

I look at every correctional officer as a truly unsung hero in our society. It was an honor for me to serve with them and I wanted them to succeed in their job and in their family life. If I could be of any help to make that happen, then I would try. The officers are there to maintain security and good order, and they look out for and protect us chaplains. They are never thanked enough by the public as they are out of sight and out of mind. They risk their lives daily for relatively low pay and often have to work overtime to make ends meet. They have nothing but a radio and their character facing 400 inmates in D block, and many of those inmates took 10 to 20 police officers just to arrest them. The officers are brave men and women.

Officers in the BOP are not the only ones who work hard. Chaplains, psychologists, education staff, and a host of other staff members work hard in the BOP. According to the Bureau of Prisons Annual Report of 2007, "approximately 38% of inmates confined by the Bureau participate in religious services or programs on a weekly basis. Nationwide, a total of 244 contractors and more than 6,600 volunteers support the work of the 252 full-time Bureau chaplains in accommodating the religious practices of more than 30 faith groups.

The Bureau's Life Connections residential multi-faith-based program attempts to transform lives and reduce recidivism. It has already reduced misconduct reports while inmates participate in the program. A recidivism analysis will take another year before enough data is available. The Thresholds Program was implemented in September 2007 and is currently operating in 31 Bureau institutions. This non-residential six-month program provides inmates with spiritual growth opportunities in key life focus areas.

In other areas in FY 07, about 23,596 inmates participated in drug abuse education courses, and some 182,317 earned an earlier release by competing strict drug abuse attendance requirements since June 1995 when the drug program began. The Bureau encourages inmates to pay court ordered fines, family support, and restitution, and they must contribute 50% of their earnings toward these obligations. In FY 07 2.7 million dollars was contributed and agency-wide about 10 million was collected through the inmate financial responsibility program. Research has found that inmates who participate in education programs at the BOP institutions are 16% less likely to recidivate and 6,907 obtained a GED certificate in FY 07. During FY 07 BOP psychologists conducted 308,142 mental health assessments/ evaluations, 50,759 individual sessions, and 2,056 crisis counseling sessions with inmates."

The Bureau of Prisons is a first class government organization that does a lot with a little. I worked in four agencies with the federal government for 24 years. LEAA as a corrections specialist—2.5 years, OAI as a program analyst—1.5 years, U.S. Parole Commission as a parole examiner—11 years, and BOP as a chaplain—9 years. I really feel the BOP was the best organization I worked for. The staff members are very professional, highly trained, skilled, and unbelievably dedicated to their jobs. I also worked in a county jail and state prison system (GA DOC) running two halfway houses, and in my opinion the BOP is really the best organization to work for.

The two BOP religious programs I would like to highlight are the Camp's Inmate Work Project and the Disciple Bible study program. They were the best that I was a part of during my tenure with the BOP. From 1989 to 1995 the Inmate Work Project went into 44 homes and involved 136 inmates who were selected for out-custody/daily furloughs to go into elderly widows' homes in downtown Atlanta and rebuild and weather strip their homes. The widows all earned less than $5000 and were selected by the volunteers in the ministry program. Materials were donated by Coca Cola, Delta Airlines and Home Depot. About six inmates went each day for two weeks to repair the widows' houses. Resource Services Ministry (RSM) volunteers in a van picked the inmates up and returned them before count time (4 p.m.) each day. RSM volunteers also supervised the inmate crew. Local churches brought lunches to the site and prayed with the inmate crew and the widow every day. This type of program is rare in corrections, but it is an opportunity for the inmate to give back, to make amends for the crime, to do a meaningful community service with some of his prison time. It was truly a wonderful program, and every inmate that participated took it seriously and did not violate the trust by stealing things from the home, meeting a woman on the sly, getting drugs delivered to him, or escaping. It was restorative justice in my opinion which I will describe in detail later.

The inmates who did the work projects told me that it was the one thing they did worthwhile during their incarceration. The widows were initially and understandably reluctant to have inmates in their home, and after two weeks of praying together, eating lunch and seeing the great work done for free on their deteriorating home, the widows were hugging the inmates and the RSM volunteers and inviting them back anytime. It was extra work for the case manager and me but satisfying work. The paperwork for the daily furlough was tough to accomplish, but the program was well worth it.

The other program I want to highlight is the Disciple program created by Bishop Richard Wilke of the Arkansas Conference. This program involves a small group of inmates in intense Bible study for

34 weeks. Reading materials and a video are purchased, and each inmate agrees to attend at least 30 of the 34 weeks to get a certificate. There is a 17-week study of the Old Testament and a 17-week study of the New Testament. I took the program with the inmates. A volunteer, Lorenzo Wright, and I were trained and certified to teach the course. It was a wonderful course, and all 12 inmates graduated. As one said, "Chaplain, this ain't no easy thing." The best Bible scholars in the country were on the videos each week, and I would guess you had to read about three hours in outside reading each week to keep up, but after it was over you had literally read 85% of the Bible.

A United Methodist Church in Acworth started Disciple Bible study the same week as we did, and we did the last 34th session together in the Prison Camp with the Acworth church (about 20 people) along with the 12 inmates who graduated in the Camp and Lorenzo and myself. Disciple I provided each inmate graduate a certificate, and he can go to a church now in his area when released and sign up for Disciple II and III. I like this kind of continuity. One inmate who was released in Tennessee attended a local church there for Disciple II and III.

The reason I liked Disciple so much was the incredible bonding that occurs in more than 34 weeks of intense, structured Bible study, and discussion. I had a feeling the inmates who attended Disciple Bible study changed, and I know I changed for the better. The study of God's word does that for you. You encounter God in His word and He bends you to His will. You feel God's loving actions moving you, and you feel His calling you to be more loving like Him. The Disciple Bible program is running in Georgia and North Carolina state prisons and perhaps others about which I do not know

This kind of love is rare in prison. I am reminded of the book and movie called *Les Miserables*. The priest is robbed of silver in his home by a thief he allowed to stay with him. When captured, the thief, Jean Valjean (Liam Neeson in the movie), is brought before the priest for justice by the police. The priest looks at the thief and tells the police that the thief broke no laws as he meant for Valjean to have the items in question. The priest tells the police that Valjean forgot to take the silver candlesticks as well and he meant for him to have them. He then gives them to him, and in the movie version he says to Liam Neeson, "I bought your soul with these candlesticks."

> The book by Victor Hugo says it better:
>
> The Bishop drew near to him, and said in a low voice: —
>
> "Do not forget, never forget, that you have promised to use this money in becoming an honest man."
>
> Jean Valjean, who had no recollection of ever having promised anything, remained speechless. The Bishop had emphasized the words when he uttered them. He resumed with solemnity: —
>
> "Jean Valjean, my brother, you no longer belong to evil, but to good. It is your soul that I buy from you; I withdraw it from black thoughts and the spirit of perdition, and I give it to God."

As I look back on the nine years, I spent at the Federal Prison Camp, Penitentiary and Detention Center Unit I want to think I facilitated Christ coming into the hearts of many of the inmates I counseled, prayed for, preached to, and offered the body and blood of Christ to during communion. Only God knows the true number who accepted the gift of Christ. I also hope many inmates of other faiths know that even though their faith is not my chosen faith that I respected theirs as much as mine. I hope some of them knew they no longer belonged to evil but to good

A few things I learned: Secure my area. Maintain security and good order in all religious programs and events. Set clear boundaries with inmates so they know what is expected and what will not be tolerated. Be fair but be firm and professional. Volunteers can accomplish more than chaplains in creating real change in inmates Training volunteers well means a lot less problems later Restorative justice occurred when fixing widow's homes in the community and is a way for inmates to make amends for their crimes. It was one of the few opportunities for inmates to pay back something to the community that was harmed. The Disciple Bible study is an excellent tool to encourage inmate change. Communion service makes things right in prison and should be offered at least once a month. As a chaplain make sure you support intelligent religious activities that do not promote a religious war. Respect and tolerate other religions.

Prior to attempting to help crime victims let us listen to what God says in the Holy Bible in the gospel according to Luke, Chapter 10:

^{25}Just then a religion scholar stood up with a question to test Jesus. "Teacher, what do I need to do to get eternal life?"
^{26}He answered, "What's written in God's Law? How do you interpret it?"
^{27}He said, "That you love the Lord your God with all your passion and prayer and muscle and intelligence—and that you love your neighbor as well as you do yourself."
^{28}"Good answer!" said Jesus. "Do it and you'll live."
^{29}Looking for a loophole, he asked, "And just how would you define 'neighbor'?"
$^{30\text{-}32}$Jesus answered by telling a story. "There was once a man traveling from Jerusalem to Jericho. On the way he was attacked by robbers. They took his clothes, beat him up, and went off leaving him half-dead. Luckily, a priest was on his way down the same road, but when he saw him he angled across to the other side. Then a Levite religious man showed up; he also avoided the injured man.
$^{33\text{-}3}$"A Samaritan traveling the road came on him. When he saw the man's condition, his heart went out to him. He gave him first aid, disinfecting and bandaging his wounds. Then he lifted him onto his donkey, led him to an inn, and made him comfortable. In the morning he took out two silver coins and gave them to the innkeeper, saying, and 'Take good care of him. If it costs any more, put it on my bill—I'll pay you on my way back.'
^{36}"What do you think? Which of the three became a neighbor to the man attacked by robbers?"
^{37}"The one who treated him kindly," the religion scholar responded.
Jesus said, "Go and do the same."
                Luke 10:25-37, The Message by Eugene Peterson

CHAPTER 3

CRIME VICTIMS CHAPLAIN

Photo by Mike DuBose, United Methodist News Service

Support Group at Vinings United Methodist Church

Being a crime victims' chaplain is a pioneer activity within the church. Crime victims have been neglected, ignored and left to fend for themselves by the church for as long as I can remember. It is a small seed trying to grow within United Methodists as it is for many other denominations. A few of us have launched out and tried to be crime victims chaplains thanks to a Restorative Justice grant from the General Board of Global Ministries. Because of that grant, I recruited, hired, trained and supervised 47 crime victims' chaplains across the USA. Several crime victims chaplains are doing some exciting ministry, such as Sandra Lydick in Fort Worth TX, Edna Morgan in Pine Bluff Arkansas, Dr. Saneta Maiko in Ft Wayne Indiana, Dr. Irv Childress in Newark NJ, David Cook in Newport Beach, Virginia, and Rev. Wayne Smith in Indiana. I stand on the shoulders of other pioneer spiritual leaders for crime victims: Janice Harris Lord and Dick Lord, Dave Delaplane, Marie Fortune, Bob Denton, Kitty Lawson, Cary Johnson, Howard Zehr, Lisa Lampman, Victims Relief chaplains in Texas and many others.

We have so far to go to even touch the surface of the spiritual needs of crime victims. They are hurting from the crimes committed against them. They are shocked numb and confused. They are angry and depressed. They feel guilt and shame from the crime. They have a crisis of faith, or temporarily or permanently lose their faith, or their faith is strengthened after the crime. They look around and see no ministry for them in this time of need because the church has not historically focused on meeting their physical—mental, emotional or spiritual needs after a serious violent crime or after a serious property crime that has left them almost broke. They may receive a brief help from clergy (a note, a phone call, a visit or funeral assistance) after the crime but when the real healing occurs months later the church is often absent.

The American Correctional Association (per Alice Heiserman) estimated that there were 8,126 local jails, state and federal, adult and juvenile, government and privatized prisons and each one with several chaplains and ministries, and when I was researching how many crime victims ministries there were in 2000 I could only find 58. I think it is close to 100 today for ministries that help crime victims. Why are we so much better as a church in ministering to the needs of those who harmed us in crimes than we are in meeting the needs of those who were harmed?

I think it is because we misread Scripture and we misunderstand the criminal justice system. The Good Samaritan parable is often quoted as a parable to help the stranger, the homeless, the addicted, and the people in need. Rarely is it ever quoted as a parable to help crime victims. The person the Good Samaritan helped was a wounded, robbed crime victim left bleeding on the side of the road. He was a crime victim. The targeted person in the story was a crime victim. He was a victim of a terrible beating and robbery, yet preachers miss this point entirely. After reviewing 25 sermons preached on the Good Samaritan story online, I only found one preacher who commented on the fact that the one helped was a crime victim. Preachers often ignore the crime victimization in the story and want to focus on helping strangers and people in need.

That Scripture convicts me daily. I wake up every day of my life and say two things, "Thy will be done . . . and Go and do thou likewise" to remind me of the end of the Good Samaritan parable. It helps me focus on the ministry of being a crime victims' chaplain and I hear Jesus' words calling me to do it; therefore, it is a warm call and one I feel called out to accept and give my life to. JESUS SAYS IF YOU LOVE ME YOU WILL OBEY MY COMMANDS AND THIS IS ONE OF HIS COMMANDS: GO AND DO THOU LIKEWISE AND TAKE THE VICTIMS TO THE INN OF HEALING (THE CHURCH) AND GIVE THEM EVERYTHING THEY NEED TO GET WELL.

Usually Christians quote the Scripture regarding visiting the sick and those in prison and say to do that because if you do that for them you do that for JESUS as well (Matthew 25: 27-36). Again, here as well we miss the meaning of that passage that a crime victim would see but others may not. When a crime victim is assaulted and put in a hospital, he or she is like a sick person. The call is to visit the sick, and those in prison and that could very well be to visit a crime victim who is like a sick person. He or she is in a hospital and is suffering mental anguish over the crime. A rape victim or victim of child molestation often says something like, "I feel like a part of me died after the crime. I felt sick. I was in a fit of rage or deep depression over the crime."

Why can we not hear the cry of the needy when they are crime victims, but we hear them cry as homeless, drug addicts, drunks, robbers, rapists, and murders? Why are we not standing with the family of the murder victims, comforting them, praying with them, and counseling them for months or years after the crime?

Perhaps it is because I have been a crime victim on so many levels that I am overly sensitive to the plight of being ignored by the church. My sister was hit in the head with a rock during the race riots in North Little Rock in 1958. My grandmother was mugged and robbed in Kansas City. I was robbed at knifepoint of 25 cents when I was 12. I lost a step-brother who was beaten to death by two men in 1977. I was burglarized in 1986. I was beaten up by bullies in school a few times when I was growing up, and I never forgot the feeling of helplessness or of being bested by an older and stronger bully.

That had something to do with why I bought a boxing bag and chose to play football. I learned to control my rage and vent it in sports. I was a skinny quarterback in high school and college, but when someone hit me with a cheap shot I would call a sweep and on a block on the next play I would hit someone with all I had. It was a flea hitting an elephant with all the flea had and it sure felt good. Every fist fight I had when growing up I lost because even when you win you lose. Your face and your hand hurt whether you win or lose, but it does seem to hurt worse when you lose. I think being bullied as a child stays with you into adulthood, and even today I cannot tolerate bullying, verbal or physical.

I had an incident in which a third grader pulled my legs out so quick I hit the playground on my face, and then he held my face in the dirt. I tried to breathe and then passed out. A friend came up afterwards and pushed the dirt out of my mouth so I could breathe and I came to. When I went to class, I had blood on my nose and lip. The teacher asked me what was wrong, and I just told her I had fallen down on the schoolyard.

About 45 years later when I was in a homicide crime victims support group, a woman asked me if I had ever been hurt as a child because I seemed to "have an edge on me" toward attackers. I seemed to get angry when discussing responses crime victims could make to attackers. Her comments bothered me all week and stayed with me. I realized she was right. I had harbored a deep-seated grudge and resentment against that nine-year-old boy who threw me down in an unprovoked attack on a playground when I was six, and I had let it simmer for 45 years. I decided to forgive that little boy for his bullying and get rid of the simmer. I will never forget it, though I can forgive him and move on. After I did that, a knot in my stomach that had been tied pretty tight for a very long time finally untied. I thank that woman in the support group for the insightful question she asked me helped me to heal from an age-old bullying assault.

I think we too often make light of schoolyard bullying and just figure boys will be boys or something like that. It affects self-image when it is being formed at an early age. It really is a crime and should be handled by school authorities before it gets out of hand and results in a serious injury. I should have told my teacher what happened and it could have been dealt with by school suspension or a paddling of the bully. I was afraid of being called a snitch or a tattletale who was such a wimp he could not solve the problem with his own wrestling or fists. That was wrong of me because the boy was much bigger and older and should have been stopped for bullying. I could have helped other boys from being hurt by the same bully. I think we need to teach young children how to stop bullies so they will not feel confused about how to respond.

All this crime victimization of muggings, bullying, murder, robbery, burglary in my own life taught me something. It taught me to fight back whether it is in the courts or the court of public opinion or the court of two fists. We had a saying in Arkansas that, "It ain't no fun when the rabbit gets the gun." The tables are turned when you fight back against your attacker and have them arrested and testify against them leading to their conviction and just sentence. It empowers you to take back that helpless feeling you had when attacked and to channel all your anger into a court battle to convict the attacker. There is a sense of relief when you win in court, but in the case of a murder or a rape there is no closure because you cannot bring back the murdered loved one and you cannot bring back yourself before the rape or murder no matter what the judicial outcome.

I really feel for the crime victims who never experience the benefit of the criminal arrested because they never have the opportunity to face down their criminal in court and receive some justice. I also feel for those crime victims who get the criminal arrested and testify in court hoping for a just outcome. After all this the criminal receives such a lenient sentence or gets off altogether on a legal loophole. Then the crime victim feels again re-victimized by the system of justice that was supposed to represent him or her. Just as bad are the DNA cases in which an attacker is proven innocent years after the conviction and now the crime victim has to wonder who the real attacker was and feels guilty for directing so much anger at the wrong person.

The field of crime victims' chaplaincy is in its infancy, and it can learn a lot from the field of criminal justice advocacy. There are over 10,000 crime victim service providers in the USA, and many of them are funded by Violence Against Women Act (VAWA) or Victims of Crime Act (VOCA). These funds come from fines from federal criminals and it gets sent to the states on a formula basis. I have learned a tremendous amount from the Victim-Witness Assistance Directors in the District Attorney's offices. After becoming close friends I will venture to say that what they are really doing is a ministry of presence with crime victims. They are filling in for the absence of the priest, the rabbi, the imam and the pastor who are not present with the crime victim in court. I have been many times to court and have yet to see the pastor sitting with the crime victim's family. I am sure somewhere a pastor or imam or rabbi is reading this and saying I was with my crime-victimized family in court, and if so I would love to hear from you because I view you as the exception and the one who is a Good Samaritan.

If you attended court as clergy with a crime victim I would like for you to send me a letter from the crime victim you went to court with, along with a witness statement from the court official who saw you there. After receiving your documents, I will ask the Crime Victims Advocacy Council, 3101 Paces Mill Rd., Atlanta, Georgia 30339 to review your application, and if you are the *first* applicant received at that address in the mail with documentation you will be selected to receive a check for $300. Use the website at www.cvaconline.org for information. You could win $300 for reading this book. I can only afford one winner. This offer will be good for two years after the date of the publishing of this book. I truly value your ministry to your crime victims and if I had more money as a retired chaplain, I would give you a higher amount.

The odd fact is that while I have not seen faith-based imams or clergy at the trial with crime victims I have seen them there testifying for the defendant as a character reference. Again I face the inequity of the system. Why would an imam, rabbi or pastor want to come to be with the person who allegedly harmed someone but not want to be present in court with those he or she harmed? I do not understand the reasons for neglecting crime victims in court.

Imagine you have been raped. The most nervous you have ever been is the day you have to go to court and sit in the same courtroom and see the person who attacked you. The offender may have threatened to kill you and your family if you testify against him. Your hand shakes as you enter the courtroom. There is no pastor there to say "Let's pray together" to calm your shaking hand. There is no pastor there to say, "I am here with you and will pray together with you for justice. I will be with you as many days as I can make it, and on other days I cannot be here I will ask someone else to come and be with you. You will not have to face this alone. I am just the hands and feet representing the care of God for you. We will not only pray for secular justice which is temporal, but we will pray for divine justice which is forever and ever. No matter what happens in this courtroom God is with you and God is the eternal judge of all that is."

That kind of pastoral presence and theological language is badly needed and very much missing in our courtrooms all over America. The faith-based community is missing a major opportunity to witness to and comfort a scared and needy soul in a trial in a courthouse and in a trial of the emotions as well. Fortunately, we have victim advocates in our courts that take the place of missing clergy or the crime victim would be totally alone if he or she did not have family or friends. Even if family or friends are around and want to come, it is difficult to take off work for very long to be in that trial which lasts for weeks. One woman was really hurt and I remember her well as she said, "I asked my pastor to come to the rape trial, but he said he was too busy. I was wondering if you could be there." I said I would be there and her face was relieved. As it turns out, the defendant pleaded guilty and she said I did not have to come to the sentencing because she had written her victim impact statement and decided not to verbalize it in court.

There is an excellent course developed by Denver Seminary for crime victims' chaplaincy and funded by the U.S. Department of Justice. Steve Siegel and Cary Johnson worked on it. It is on our CVAC website, www.cvaconline.org. Any seminary can access it and use it for training pastors in seminary. Dave Delaplane, and Janice Harris Lloyd also developed training material on crime victims' spiritual care. I developed some crime victim's chaplaincy training, which can be found on www.youtube.org/cvaconline. Dr. Marie Fortune has developed some very good training on faith-based work with domestic violence. Victims Relief in Texas is an organization that trains and certifies crime victims' chaplains as emergency responders after a crime. Victims Relief chaplains is another resource.

International Critical Incident Stress Foundation (ICISF) has a good training on pastoral crisis intervention after a crime. My seminary, Drew Theological School, added a course in chaplaincy and pastoral care in their curriculum. Drew Seminary's Dean, Maxine Beach, asked me to provide training in crime victims' ministry during Tipple Vosburgh lectures. Rev. Patricia Barrett, Assistant General Secretary for United Methodist Endorsing Agency, taught some coursework on chaplaincy at Drew, but it mostly dealt with general issues of chaplaincy and hospital chaplaincy.

CHAPTER 4

FORGIVENESS

Tom Porter of JustPeace wrote a piece entitled "Engage Conflict Well, and in it he states the following:

Be forgiving.

For if you forgive others their trespasses, your heavenly Father will also forgive you: but if you do not forgive others, neither will your Father forgive your trespasses" (Mt 6:14-15). "Then Peter came and said to him, 'Lord, if another member of the church sins against me, how often should I forgive? As many as seven times?' Jesus said to him, 'Not seven times, but, I tell you, seventy-seven times'" (Mt 18:21-22).

Forgiveness is a craft that needs to be learned. It is an embodied way of life. Each day it must be prayed for and struggled for and won (see L. Gregory Jones).

Forgiveness is where the victim of some hurtful action freely chooses to release the perpetrator of that action from the bondage of guilt, gives up his or her own feelings of ill will, and surrenders any attempt to hurt or damage the perpetrator in return, thus clearing the way for reconciliation and restoration of relationship" (Christopher Marshall).

Forgiveness is not weakness, the excusing of wrong, denial, forgetfulness, or automatic" (Christopher Marshall).

The dynamics of forgiveness involve acknowledging the situation needing forgiveness, deciding to enter the forgiveness cycle, giving voice to the pain and anger, being open to the offender, being willing to experience the 'fellowship of sufferings,' forgiving other parties, becoming reconciled with the past, and becoming reconciled with the person" (Christopher Marshall).

Blessed are those who are willing to enter into the process
of being healed,
for they will become healers.
Blessed are those who recognize their own inner
violence,
for they will come to know nonviolence.
Blessed are those who can forgive self,
for they will become forgivers.
Blessed are those who are willing to let go
of selfishness and self-centeredness,
for they will become a healing presence.
Blessed are those who listen with compassion,
for they will become compassionate.
Blessed are those who are willing to enter into conflict,
for they will find transformation.
Blessed are those who know their interdependence with
all of creation,
for they will become unifiers.
Blessed are those who live a contemplative life stance,
for they will find God in all things.
Blessed are those who strive to live these beatitudes,
for they will be reconcilers.

Sisters of St. Joseph of Concordia
Mediation and Facilitation Training Manual

Mennonite Conciliation Service

Be a truth and reconciliation person...for whom every meeting, every utterance, every gesture is about truth and about reconciliation. First, be about truth:

Truth about wonder and about wound

Truth about race and gender

Truth about money and power

Truth about not caring and not noticing

Truth that makes us free, about the self-giving God and the self-giving community.

The truth that losing is gaining and keeping is losing, that emptying is the only way to fullness.

The truth that forgiveness is possible.

And only then be about reconciliation: In quite concrete places.

That, as the result of truth telling, heals and lets the past be past, for the sake of new embrace.

Walter Brueggemann

Tom Porter's JustPeace and the quotations above indicate how his organization helps congregations in conflict after a crime like sexual assault or harassment takes place in a church. It is a valuable resource and can help churches heal after the crime. Another excellent resource is Dr. Michael Christensen's Shalom Zone that attempts to create Shalom Zones in urban areas and can be a source for crime victim's chaplains to receive funding and technical assistance when they are getting started. The Office for Victims of Crime (OVC Hope grants) and the General Board of Global Ministry (Community Action grants and Restorative Justice grants) can also provide financial assistance for new chaplains. Funding is difficult for a community-based chaplaincy and local churches have funds in missions committees to help a new crime victim's ministry.

As victims of crime, we can speak the truth to each other within the context of a support group, and engage in the healing process. We first have to admit that this crime hurt us deeply and we do not know how to cope with it. We see answers but we are usually living out and clarifying the right questions. We need somewhere safe and confidential where we can tell our stories to each other about what crime brought us to the point of needing this kind of help in a support group. We need others to listen deeply and to care about us and our pain and grief. We need to feel and sense the struggle of the entire group in order to work on making us better instead of bitter. Each member of the group is equal in the ability to share and respect one another's comments. Each member of the group is equal in the ability to share and respect one another's comments. Each member can help each other clarify their true feelings even when the one speaking cannot see the real feelings. The healing is always a work in progress but one worth taking.

Forgiveness is different when a serious crime has occurred than it is for a neighbor's slight or unkind word or even a spouse's criticism. Imagine a young child molested by a family friend. A daughter raped and murdered. A daughter scared out of her mind because of terroristic stalking. An elderly mother stripped of all her life savings by a con man who defrauded her. It asks so much more of the victim in these types of circumstances. Because of consequences that will affect his appeals if he admits guilt the offender seldom asks for forgiveness, repents, or exhibits remorse. It is hard to forgive someone who never asks for it or who never tells you he is sorry for what he did.

I think our society has to be graceful here and not rush our crime victims to start forgiving before they are even in the process of dealing with grieving or healing. They may never forgive the offender, and that is their right. As a pastoral counselor we can only be a listener, a co-journeyer and a facilitator for their journey. We cannot and should not "make them" forgive.

The Oxford English Dictionary defines forgiveness as "to grant free pardon and to give up all claim on account of an offence or debt." *Wikipedia* states that

"Forgiveness is typically defined as the process of concluding resentment, indignation or anger as a result of a perceived offense, difference or mistake, and/or ceasing to demand punishment or restitution. The concept and benefits of forgiveness have been explored in religious thought, medicine, and the social sciences. Forgiveness may be considered simply in terms of the person who forgives including forgiving themselves, in terms of the person forgiven and/or in terms of the relationship between the forgiver and the person forgiven. In some contexts, forgiveness may be granted without any expectation of restorative justice, and without any response on the part of the offender (for example, one may forgive a person who is incommunicado or dead). In practical terms, it may be necessary for the offender to offer some form of acknowledgment, apology, and/or restitution, or even just ask for forgiveness, in order for the wronged person to believe he is able to forgive.

Most world religions include teaching on the nature of forgiveness, and many of those teachings provide an underlying basis for many varying modern day traditions and practices of forgiveness. Some religious doctrines or philosophies place greater emphasis on the need for humans to find some sort of divine forgiveness for their own shortcomings, others make little or no distinction between human and divine forgiveness.

Prior to the 1980s, forgiveness was a practice primarily left to matters of faith. Although there is presently no consensus psychological definition of forgiveness in the research literature, agreement has emerged that forgiveness is a process and a number of models describing the process of forgiveness have been published, including one from a radical behavioral perspective.

Dr. Robert Enright from the University of Wisconsin–Madison founded the International Forgiveness Institute and is considered the initiator of forgiveness studies. He developed a 20-Step Process Model of Forgiveness. Recent work has focused on what kind of person is more likely to be forgiving. A longitudinal study showed that people who were generally more neurotic, angry and hostile in life were less likely to forgive another person even after a long time had passed. Specifically, these people were more likely to still avoid their transgressor and want to enact revenge upon them four and a half years after the transgression.

Studies show that people who forgive are happier and healthier than those who hold resentments. The first study to look at how forgiveness improves physical health discovered that when people think about forgiving an offender it leads to improved functioning in their cardiovascular and nervous systems. Another study at the University of Wisconsin found the more forgiving people were, the less they suffered from a wide range of illnesses. The less forgiving people reported a greater number of health problems.

The research of Dr. Fred Luskin of Stanford University shows that forgiveness can be learned. In three separate studies, including one with Catholics and Protestants from Northern Ireland whose family members were murdered in the political violence, he found that people who are less hurt are more optimistic, become more forgiving in a variety of situations, and become more compassionate and self-confident. His studies show a reduction in experience of stress, physical manifestations of stress, and an increase in vitality.

One study has shown that the positive benefit of forgiveness is similar whether it was based upon religious or secular counseling as opposed to a control group who received no forgiveness counseling."

As a Christian pastoral counselor I viewed forgiveness as part of the journey crime victims make in their healing process. When they wanted to deal with it, they would bring it up in family, individual or group sessions with me as a crime victim's chaplain. I stated I was a "co-journeyer" with them and was not the final authority on the matter. I referred them to the Bible to read about forgiveness and to several books by Christian authors. I asked them to state what they felt about forgiveness at that moment. If we were in a group I asked everyone to weigh in on what they thought. Several members of the group would quote the Lord's Prayer that teaches us to ask God to forgive us of our own trespasses as we forgive others who have trespassed us against us. I stressed that what is important is how the crime victim feels about the subject right now. I tried to listen deeply to the "words and feelings behind the words" and hear where the crime victim was in that moment so I could reflect the congruent feelings. I made no value judgments and let her know I understood how she felt about forgiveness. Only then could we move forward together.

Wikipedia states:

In the New Testament, Jesus speaks of the importance of Christians forgiving or showing mercy towards others. The Parable of the Prodigal Son is perhaps the best known instance of such teaching and practice of forgiveness.

In the Sermon on the Mount, Jesus repeatedly spoke of forgiveness, "Blessed are the merciful, for they will be shown mercy." Matthew 5:7 (NIV) "Therefore, if you are offering your gift at the altar and there remember that your brother has something against you, leave your gift there in front of the altar. First go and be reconciled to your brother; then come and offer your gift." Matthew 5:23-24 (NIV) "And when you stand praying, if you hold anything against anyone, forgive him, so that your Father in heaven may forgive you your sins." Mark 11:25 (NIV) "But I tell you who hear me: Love your enemies, do good to those who hate you, bless those who curse you, pray for those who mistreat you. If someone strikes you on one cheek, turn to him the other also." Luke 6:27-29 (NIV) "Be merciful, just as your Father is merciful." Luke 6:36 (NIV) "Do not judge, and you will not be judged. Do not condemn, and you will not be condemned. Forgive, and you will be forgiven." Luke 6:37 (NIV)

Elsewhere, it is said, "Then Peter came and said to Him, 'Lord, how often shall my brother sin against me and I forgive him? Up to seven times?" Jesus said to him, 'I do not say to you, up to seven times, but up to seventy times seven.'" Matthew 18:21-22 (NAS)

Jesus asked for God's forgiveness of the Romans who crucified him. "And Jesus said, 'Father, forgive them, for they know not what they do.'" Luke 23: 34 (ESV)

On a personal level I found the most freeing statement on forgiveness to come from Howard Zehr in *Changing Lenses* when he said forgiveness was "letting go of the power the offense and the offender has over you in your life," and I would add letting go of the intensity it has as well. This untied my own knots in my stomach that lay there repressed for years after my stepbrother was murdered. I did let go and it was a tremendous relief. I do not presume this will be the case for everyone, but it was for me.

These various theories about forgiveness demonstrate to me that each person needs to formulate their own views about the subject and that their views will be shaped by their religious beliefs, family traditions and cultural norms. I stress that their views about forgiving an offender of an egregious act should come when the victims are ready and not be forced upon them before they are.

Wikipedia states:

Bahá'í

"In the Bahá'í Writings, this explanation is given of how to be forgiving towards others:

"Love the creatures for the sake of God and not for themselves. You will never become angry or impatient if you love them for the sake of God. Humanity is not perfect. There are imperfections in every human being, and you will always become unhappy if you look toward the people themselves. But if you look toward God, you will love them and be kind to them, for the world of God is the world of perfection and complete mercy. Therefore, do not look at the shortcomings of anybody; see with the sight of forgiveness."
— `Abdu'l-Bahá, *The Promulgation of Universal Peace*, p. 92

Buddhism

In Buddhism, forgiveness is seen as a practice to prevent harmful thoughts from causing havoc on one's mental well-being. Buddhism recognizes that feelings of hatred and ill-will leave a lasting effect on our mind karma. Instead, Buddhism encourages the cultivation of thoughts that leave a wholesome effect. "In contemplating the law of karma, we realize that it is not a matter of seeking revenge but of practicing *metta* and forgiveness, for the victimizer is, truly, the most unfortunate of all. When resentments have already arisen, the Buddhist view is to calmly proceed to release them by going back to their roots. Buddhism centers on release from delusion and suffering through meditation and receiving insight into the nature of reality. Buddhism questions the reality of the passions that make forgiveness necessary as well as the reality of the objects of those passions "If we haven't forgiven, we keep creating an identity around our pain, and that is what is reborn. That is what suffers."

Buddhism places much emphasis on the concepts of *mettā* (loving kindness), *karuna* (compassion), *mudita* (sympathetic joy), and *upekkhā* (equanimity), as a means to avoiding resentments in the first place. These reflections are used to understand the context of suffering in the world, both our own and the suffering of others.

"He abused me, he struck me, he overcame me, he robbed me'—in those who harbor such thoughts hatred will never cease."

"He abused me, he struck me, he overcame me, he robbed me'—in those who do not harbor such thoughts hatred will cease."

(Dhammapada 1.3-4; trans. Radhakrishnan)

Hinduism

The concept of performing atonement from one's wrongdoing (Prayaschitta— Sanskrit: Penance), and asking for forgiveness is very much a part of the practice of Hinduism. Prayashitta is related to the law of Karma. Karma is a sum of all that an individual has done, is currently doing, and will do. The effects of those deeds and these deeds actively create present and future experiences, thus making one responsible for one's own life, and the pain in others.

Addressing Dhritarashtra, Vidura said: "There is one only defect in forgiving persons, and not another; that defect is that people take a forgiving person to be weak. That defect, however, should not be taken into consideration, for forgiveness is a great power. Forgiveness is a virtue of the weak, and an ornament of the strong. Forgiveness subdues (all) in this world; what is there that forgiveness cannot achieve? What can a wicked person do unto him who carries the sabre of forgiveness in his hand? Fire falling on the grassless ground is extinguished of itself. And unforgiving individual defiles himself with many enormities. Righteousness is the one highest good; and forgiveness is the one supreme peace; knowledge is one supreme contentment; and benevolence, one sole happiness." (From the Mahabharata, Udyoga Parva Section XXXIII, Translated by Sri Kisari Mohan Ganguli).

An even more authoritative statement about forgiveness is espoused by Krishna, who is considered to be an incarnation (*avatar*) of Vishnu by Hindus. Krishna said in the Gita that forgiveness is one of the characteristics of one born for a divine state. It is noteworthy that he distinguishes those good traits from those he considered to be demoniac, such as pride, self-conceit and anger (Bhagavad Gita, Chapter 16, verse 3).

Village priests may open their temple ceremonies with the following beloved invocation:

O Lord, forgive three sins that are due to my human limitations: Thou art everywhere, but I worship you here; Thou art without form, but I worship you in these forms; Thou needest no praise, yet I offer you these prayers and salutations, Lord, forgive three sins that are due to my human limitations.

Islam

Islam teaches that God (Allah in Arabic) is 'the most forgiving', and is the original source of all forgiveness. Forgiveness often requires the repentance of those being forgiven. Depending on the type of wrong committed, forgiveness can come either directly from Allah, or from one's fellow man who received the wrong. In the case of divine forgiveness, the asking for divine forgiveness via repentance is important. In the case of human forgiveness, it is important to both forgive, and to be forgiven.

The Qur'an makes it clear that, whenever possible, it is better to forgive another than to attack another. The Qur'an describes the believers (Muslims) as those who, *avoid gross sins and vice, and when angered they forgive.* (Qur'an 42:37) and says that *Although the just requital for an injustice is an equivalent retribution, those who pardon and maintain righteousness are rewarded by GOD. He does not love the unjust. (Qur'an 42:40).*

To receive forgiveness from God there are three requirements:

    1. Recognizing the offense itself and its admission before God.

2. Making a commitment not to repeat the offense.

3. Asking for forgiveness from God.

If the offense was committed against another human being, or against society, a fourth condition is added:

1. Recognizing the offense before those against whom offense was committed and before God.

2. Committing oneself not to repeat the offense.

3. Doing whatever needs to be done to rectify the offense (within reason) and asking pardon of the offended party.

4. Asking God for forgiveness.

Jainism

In Jainism, forgiveness is one the main virtues that needs to be cultivated by the Jains. *Kṣamāpanā* or supreme forgiveness forms part of one of the ten characteristics of *dharma*. In the Jain prayer (*pratikramana*) Jains repeatedly seek forgiveness from various creatures—even from *ekindriyas* or single sensed beings like plants and microorganisms that they may have harmed while eating and doing routine activities. Forgiveness is asked by uttering the phrase, *Micchāmi dukkaḍaṃ*. *Micchāmi dukkaḍaṃ* is a prakrit phrase literally meaning "may all the evil that has been done be fruitless." During *samvatsari*—the last day of Jain festival *paryusana*—Jains utter the phrase *Micchami Dukkadam* after *pratikraman*. As a matter of ritual, they personally greet their friends and relatives *micchāmi dukkaḍaṃ* seeking their forgiveness. No private quarrel or dispute may be carried beyond samvatsari, and letters and letters and telephone calls are made to the outstation friends and relatives asking their forgiveness.

Jain texts quote Māhavīra on forgiveness:

By practicing *prāyaṣcitta* (repentance), a soul gets rid of sins, and commits no transgressions; he who correctly practises *prāyaṣcitta* gains the road and the reward of the road, he wins the reward of good conduct. By begging forgiveness he obtains happiness of mind; thereby he acquires a kind disposition towards all kinds of living beings; by this kind disposition he obtains purity of character and freedom from fear.

Judaism

In Judaism, if a person causes harm, but then sincerely and honestly apologizes to the wronged individual and tries to rectify the wrong, the wronged individual is religiously required to grant forgiveness:

"It is forbidden to be obdurate and not allow yourself to be appeased. On the contrary, one should be easily pacified and find it difficult to become angry. When asked by an offender for forgiveness, one should forgive with a sincere mind and a willing spirit . . . forgiveness is natural to the seed of Israel." (Mishneh Torah, *Teshuvah* 2:10)

In Judaism, one must go *to those he has harmed* in order to be entitled to forgiveness. One who sincerely apologizes three times for a wrong committed against another has fulfilled his or her obligation to seek forgiveness. (Shulchan Aruch) OC 606:1] This means that, unlike in Christianity, in Judaism a person cannot obtain forgiveness from God for wrongs the person has done to other people. Thus the *Tefila Zaka* meditation, which is recited just before Yom Kippur, closes with the following:

"I know that there is no one so righteous that they have not wronged another, financially or physically, through deed or speech. This pains my heart within me, because wrongs between humans and their fellow are not atoned by Yom Kippur, until the wronged one is appeased. Because of this, my heart breaks within me, and my bones tremble; for even the day of death does not atone for such sins. Therefore I prostrate and beg before You to have mercy on me, and grant me grace, compassion, and mercy in Your eyes and in the eyes of all people. For behold, I forgive with a final and resolved forgiveness anyone who has wronged me, whether in person or property, even if they slandered me, or spread falsehoods against me. So I release anyone who has injured me either in person or in property, or has committed any manner of sin that one may commit against another [except for legally enforceable business obligations, and except for someone who has deliberately harmed me with the thought 'I can harm him because he will forgive me']. Except for these two, I fully and finally forgive everyone; may no one be punished because of me. And just as I forgive everyone, **so may You grant me grace in the eyes of others, that they too forgive me absolutely**."

Thus the "reward" for forgiving others is not God's forgiveness for wrongs done to others, but rather help *in obtaining forgiveness from the other person*.

Sir Jonathan Sacks, Chief Rabbi of the United Hebrew Congregations of the Commonwealth, summarized: "it is not that God forgives, while human beings do not. To the contrary, we believe that just as only God can forgive sins against God, so only human beings can forgive sins against human beings."

Jews observe a Day of Atonement Yom Kippur on the day before God makes decisions regarding what will happen during the coming year. Just prior to Yom Kippur, Jews will ask forgiveness of those they have wronged during the prior year (if they have not already done so). During Yom Kippur itself, Jews fast and pray for God's forgiveness for the transgressions they have made against God in the prior year. Sincere repentance is required, and once again, God can only forgive one for the sins one has committed against God; this is why it is necessary for Jews also to seek the forgiveness of those people who they have wronged.[7]

Ho'oponopono

Ho'oponopono (ho-o-pono-pono) is an ancient Hawaiian practice of reconciliation and forgiveness, combined with prayer. Similar forgiveness practices were performed on islands throughout the South Pacific, including Samoa, Tahiti and New Zealand. Traditionally ho'oponopono is practiced by healing priests or *kahuna lapa'au* among family members of a person who is physically ill. Modern versions are performed within the family by a family elder, or by the individual alone."

I would venture to say that every person in the USA is a victim of crime. I would also say there are three kinds of crime victims: past, present, and future. After September 11, 2001 we all felt victimized by the terrorist crimes against the Pentagon, World Trade Center and an aborted attempt in Pennsylvania. Not one person was free from seeing the images on television of our fellow Americans cut down by terrorists. There is a military and a law enforcement response to find and prosecute these terrorists who killed innocent Americans and foreigners. I also think we as clergy should have an educational and theological response that seeks to work toward peace and harmony of different religions. We should respect and tolerate other religions but if the extremists want to kill us they should be stopped at all costs. I will never forget September 11. I am working on the process of forgiving myself for not doing more than one week of counseling in NYC to help the surviving family members of that attack.

Chapter 5

The National Crime Victims Rights Week Resource Guide of 2009 Provides a Good Overview of Crime in our Nation

In 2006, 25 million crimes were committed in the United States; of these, 6 million were violent and 19 million were property crimes. Forty-nine percent of violent crime and 38 percent of property crime were reported to the police. An estimated 16,929 persons were murdered nationwide in 2007, a six percent decline from 2006. Child protective services nationwide found an estimated 905,000 children to be victims of neglect or abuse in 2006. In 2006, 606,350 women and 148,460 men were victimized by an intimate partner. In 2006, victims experienced 272,350 incidents of rape and sexual assault. More than one million women and almost 400,000 men are stalked annually in the United States. In 2006, teens ages 12 to 19 and young adults ages 20 to 24 experienced the highest rates of violent crime. In 2006, teens ages 12 to 19 experienced 1.7 million violent crimes. More than a quarter of people with severe mental illness had been victims of a violent crime in the past year, a rate more than 11 times higher than that of the general population, even after controlling for demographic differences.

- Of the 41,059 deaths in motor vehicle crashes in 2007, 31 percent, or 12,998, were attributed to alcohol.

- In 2006, 117,760 persons over the age of 65 were victims of nonfatal violent crime.

- In 2006, 7,722 hate crimes were reported to law enforcement.

- Between 2003 and 2007, the number of adult victims of identity fraud in the United States declined from 10 million to 8.4 million people.

- In 2006, 25 percent of all violent crime incidents were committed by an armed offender, and nine percent by an offender with a firearm.

- Each year, an estimated 4,500 to 17,500 foreign nationals are trafficked into the United States.

- In 2006, 773,244 persons were victims of violent crime while working or on duty. Of these incidents, 589,763 (76 percent) were simple assaults while an additional 17 percent were aggravated assaults.

- Sixteen percent of violent crime and 94 percent of property crime resulted in economic losses in 2006.

- In 2007, 88,040 crimes were reported on college and university campuses; of these, 97 percent were property crimes, and 3 percent were violent crimes.

- In 2005, students ages 12 to 18 were victims of 136,500 serious violent crimes at school.

These statistics do not tell the stories of the millions of people hurt by criminals, nor are these facts as comprehensive as they need to be. If, for example, we take the 16,929 murders in 2007 alone and use a range of 15,000 to 17,000 murdered every year for the last 10 years, that is 150,000 to 170,000 of us murdered in the USA in the last decade. If we just take just six immediate family members (grandmother grandfather mother father son and daughter) connected to each murder and do not count close friends or cousins or aunts and uncles or nephews and nieces affected by these murders, then six x 150,000 adds up to 900,000 or almost a million of us grieving over the loss of a loved one killed by a murderer in the last decade. Add friends and cousins, nephews, nieces, aunts and uncles and close coworkers and it is astronomical how many people are affected by murder in our country.

The clergy are trained in seminary to pray with grieving families over a loss, to conduct funerals and memorials, to counsel those who are grieving. But if you asked a clergyman what the amount of victims compensation is for a murder in his or her state you would draw a blank. If you walked into a clergyman's office and asked for help in writing the parole board about a parole hearing, or how to file a victim impact statement to get restitution, or who should be contacted for a civil justice tort claim based on the crime you would draw a blank stare. I would hope if more crime victims asked their clergy to go to court with them at the trial that more clergy would go and therefore become educated in crime victimization.

I would want to see faith-based organizations implement real justice in our land. Require seminaries to teach a course on criminal justice and mercy ministries and Restorative Justice. Train and endorse as many crime victims' chaplains as prison chaplains. It could be part of a course on chaplaincy or it could be the entire course curriculum similar to the one at Denver Seminary. The Office of Victims of Crime, USDOJ, paid to develop this Denver Seminary course and we should be using it.

Perhaps OVC could fund the program cost in at least one seminary in each major denomination to pioneer the Denver Seminary model to get it started. OVC could offer Hope I or Hope II grants to get crime victims chaplains started in their communities. This is how crime victims' chaplains Edna Morgan of Pine Bluff Arkansas, Sandra Lydick of Fort Worth, Texas, Irv Childress of Newark, New Jersey, Wayne Smith and Saneta Maiko in Indiana got started. They received start-up funding from OVC Hope grants.

In the event of another mass terrorism (hopefully not) event like 9/11 we will need trained and prepared crime victims chaplains to come to the aid of surviving crime victims. It is better to be prepared and never needed than to be unprepared and to use hastily thrown together volunteer chaplains like we did after 9/11. We should continue and expand the existing training developed by OVC for *Mental Health Response to Mass Violence and Terrorism, (NCJRS 205451)* and have each Governor appoint 50 chaplains to attend which would give us 2500 trained chaplains.

At the federal level we should have a trained and certified crime victims chaplain on contract to serve each US Attorney VWAP's Office and on call to serve the FBI Victims advocate. The contract for the crime victims' chaplain can be offered by competitive bid. A full-time crime victims chaplain would oversee the hiring by contract of each chaplain in each local office of the US Attorney VWAP, similar to the way the Bureau of Prisons Central Office chaplains supervises all chaplains in federal correctional institutions. This should also be coordinated by the Office of Faith-Based Programs at the White House.

There is a strong need for crime victim education at the local church, synagogue and mosque, and materials need to be developed on prison ministry, restorative justice and crime victims' advocacy at the Sunday School level in mainline faith-based organizations, and in synagogue and mosque educational programs. In fact, some work has been done, and I contributed to a publication called *Restorative Justice: Moving Beyond Punishment* published by the United Methodist Church and authored by Harmon Wray in 2002 (ISBN#1-890569-34-8). We were able to get it to be recommended for study by all United Methodist Sunday Schools a few years ago. We took the materials in the book and trained several hundred United Methodists in five regional trainings across the country. The Presbyterians published *Justice or "Just Deserts"?* in December 2001.

Dr. Mark Umbreit of Minnesota and Dr. Howard Zehr of Virginia have pioneered the way for faith-based organizations to understand and use restorative justice principles in victim-offender mediated groups. I like the application of victim-offender mediation when the crime is non-violent and especially for juveniles.

When a serious injury has occurred, I am against efforts to coerce a crime victim to meet with the victim who harmed them; however gently the suggestion to "use restorative justice as an option" is made. I also do not think some victim offender mediations are victim-centric enough because I believe *in every criminal case in which the crime costs money for the victim* the offender should pay in restitution and community service hours and pay into that victim's fund.

Traditionally, we have allowed the offender too much latitude in making the monthly restitution payments resulting in a "nickel to half dollar paid on the dollar owed" or no payments made at all with no consequence. I would suggest that every convicted person who has financial resources and does not make a diligent effort to pay restitution should be evaluated to determine if he should be placed in a halfway house by the court or paroling authority for 60 to 120 days. I would also suggest we improve our protocols in finding crime victims who are owed restitution but move without notifying the probation/parole officer or leave no forwarding address. In these days of Internet searches we should be able to find most crime victims to send them their court-ordered or parole-ordered restitution payments.

Chapter 6

THE THREE R's:
RECONCILIATION, REDEMPTION & RESTORATION

A new theology in our schools of theological education would deal with crime and justice from the central point of view of the crime victim. The crime victim could be the prisoner who was abused, the actual victim of the prisoner, or the community that has been abused by the crime. The theology would touch on systematic theology of reconciliation, redemption and restoration. It would cross over into many other departments of Christian or faith-based ethics, pastoral care, church history, world religions, and philosophy (particularly the problem of theodicy (good versus evil, judgment, and concepts of eternal punishment). Even Denver Seminary, which is the best curriculum I have found for crime victims chaplains in seminary, primarily deals with crime victims' advocacy and barely deals with some of these theological topics.

It would be highly instructional during the class study for students and faculty to hear from crime victims who have experienced a murder or rape or armed robbery. To hear from a person willing to give a testimony to the class about the experience would be invaluable in teaching the students a level of crime victims' awareness and sensitivity that is not presently found in our seminaries. Randy McCall of VAONLINE in Canada has taped testimonies of victim impact statements, and they can be accessed on the Internet if it is difficult to find crime victims willing to come to a seminary class. To hear the shock, numbness and confusion, the anger and depression, the guilt and shame that come from the heart and feelings of crime victims after a traumatic crime is the best form of educating future pastors on this topic. To hear how nervous the crime victim was in court and to hear how the system sometimes re-victimized them by the way they are marginalized is important knowledge that may someday make a pastor want to go to court and hold the hands and pray with the crime victim who has been harmed and is a member of his congregation.

It involves ethics on all levels. Which laws are just and fair for all the people and which laws are fair for the dominant group but not so fair for the minorities? Is it right to ask for a particular sentence for a rich, white person who was harmed and ask for a different sentence for a poor, minority person who was harmed? Can the victim speak to the offender and hear the offender's apology before or after the conviction? Can the victim receive all the rights the state ensures (participate and be heard in court and at parole, information, notification, compensation, to name a few) similar to the offender receiving all his rights under the state, such as Miranda, disclosure, right of appeal and to cross examine?

Is it ethical to incarcerate more blacks than whites based on economic class and race and status in the community? Is racial profiling ethical? Being arrested for driving while Black? Is it right to focus so much attention on street crime that steals a few million from us when less focus is placed on white collar criminals who pollute streams and the air that kill us or defraud us of billions like Ken Lay or Jeff Skilling of Enron, or Bernie Madoff?

Was it right to make severe penalties for crack cocaine sold cheaply in minority neighborhoods and establish much less severe sentences for powdered cocaine sold in upper class neighborhoods? Is it right to selectively enforce laws against the poor or people of color? Is it ethical for state or federally supported chaplains to allow abuses rather than confront them for which they may be fired? Once these questions are framed and asked, it causes a critical re-evaluation of the fairness and equity of our history of inflicting retribution or punishment.

Pastoral care for crime victims could include techniques of emergency response such as a prison chaplain, police chaplain, hospital chaplain and disaster chaplain encounters soon after the crime. Mid-to-long term pastoral counseling of crime victims will involve individual, family and group sessions like in a weekly support group usually held in the faith-based organization's facility. Knowledge of how to identify and treat Post Traumatic Stress Disorder, prisoners or crime victims with mental or physical disability, and those dying of injuries inflicted by the criminal or those dying of a disease, like AIDS, TB or cancer in prison. A clergy's knowledge of basic crime victims' rights in each state are crucial to help a crime victim heal by exercising their rights. Clergy can take the OVC course, called Victim Assistance Training or VAT online, in order to understand victim advocacy better.

Understanding church history, theology of salvation (soteriology), the history of jurisprudence, criminology and victimology informs who we are now with respect to our concept of punishment. When man first disobeys God and eats at the tree of the knowledge of good and evil it all starts to unfold. Man can choose to obey or disobey God, and when he disobeys God and goes against God's law he chooses evil and suffers painful consequences such as banishment from the Garden of Eden. Paul and Jesus were thrown into prison and the early church apostles suffered persecution for their religion and martyrdom, except for John who died an old man. Moses killed two of pharaoh's men, and King David had an officer in his army placed in harm's way to gain the officer's wife for himself. Cain slew Abel out of jealousy. Most crimes are committed from need, greed, jealousy or revenge, and the Bible is full of these stories.

Jurisprudence in this country is heavily influenced by its origination in the King's law in England. The most significant development has been the way the state is now in many ways similar to the King who looks out for justice to be delivered. The prosecutor and the defense counsel go to war for the state to convict or exonerate the defendant. The crime victim is marginalized and often told it is best to accept a plea rather than face a not guilty possibility. As crime victims we are intimidated by an experienced prosecutor and "go along to get along," with the hopes the prosecutor will be successful in court with a good conviction that will stand up on appeal. Crime victims are not lawyers and are sometimes too scared to object to the prosecuting lawyer's strategy or to alienate them. Power and respect are all on the state prosecutor's side and crime victims have very little power or respect in the process of the courtroom drama that unfolds like a boring Perry Mason show. If, for example, we (the crime victims) asked the prosecutor to let us work it out with the defendant, in most cases he would laugh. We would be asking him to relinquish the power to prosecute and that is his primary role and job.

Restorative justice models do just that; ask the prosecutor to let the victims and offenders work it out. I had a good friend whose church was vandalized by a teenager who destroyed the pastor's and church secretary's computer and put graffiti on the walls that looked satanic even though the boy was not a member of a satanic cult. He did it as a lark, but the church was extremely angry at what they thought was an attack by a Satanist. The boy was caught and given two years probation, and the church people did not go to the trial. I would have liked to see the boy ordered to pay restitution by washing cars for the church people every Saturday for a year. I would like to see the boy ordered to do community service by repainting the walls he destroyed, and mow the church lawn for a year. I would like to have the pastor and church secretary and a representative member of the congregation sit down in a family conference with the boy and his mother and father, guardians, or significant relatives, and discuss how this crime made them feel. The trained mediator could be a probation officer or a restorative justice victim-offender mediator, a trained police officer, a police chaplain, or a crime victim's chaplain. The boy could be invited, but not coerced, to attend church at the facility he harmed so the entire church could meet him and offer him Christ's love and a dose of reality about how they felt as victims of his actions. If he completed lawn mowing, wall painting and car washing, and attended family conferencing as agreed, he would not have a criminal record in a diversion program. If he did not want to do this, he could go the traditional route to court and receive a just verdict and sentence (two years probation) for what he did.

If I had talked to the church pastor in time, I would have recommended all of the above mediation in place of traditional court action. I asked the pastor how he felt after the two year probated sentence was given to the boy, and he said he was still angry that the boy used Satanic symbols. He did not go to the boy's trial because the boy was a juvenile and not Satanic, and he figured it was up to the state to prosecute him. In a mediated family conference these feelings of anger and not feeling satisfied with the impersonal judicial process could have been shared and dealt with by all parties present. I particularly like the talking stick approach, which has Native American roots. Each member of the group sits in a circle and holds a sacred object and talks out how they feel, and when finished they pass the stick to the next person. No one interrupts or asks a question or makes a statement but just deeply listens to the "words behind the words" or true meaning of what is being said. Over many years I have found it to be a real aid to healing.

In short, I am recommending a form of family group conferencing that has been done in Wagga Australian groups, New Zealand Maori groups, and several other places around the globe. I think the Native American talking stick is a healing tool to encourage all parties to talk the conflict over in order to come to some collective resolution. This form of ritual shaming and instilling guilt by conferencing all parties involved leads to reconciliation of broken relationships. It restores shalom or peace that was disturbed by the crime. It may or may not lead to a sincere remorse and an apology by the offender to the victim, but hopefully, an apology and a request to be forgiven will be forthcoming from the offender through the discussions in the conference. A sincere heart-felt forgiveness from the victim to the offender may or may not come from the effort, but, hopefully when one encounters the offender in person and sees he is not the terrible monster as originally envisioned, a form of the forgiveness process will be begun.

Reconciliation is a religious term used in soteriology, the study of salvation. How a person is "saved" today is over laden with liberal and conservative views. I know that we have not been "saving" inmates very often because the system is set up to punish, not save. We label and stigmatize a juvenile as a deviant when we lock him up, and he rarely has the capacity to break the brand. We place him with other so-called deviants and he learns more crime and further hardens his criminal mentality, self-image and deviant behaviors. He now begins to take pride in being a criminal. By doing a family group conference as a diversion program we can avoid the labeling and stigmatizing, and build up feelings of shame and guilt for wrongful acts that may lead to less re-offending.

Criminologists never seem to agree on causes of crime. They discuss lack of internal control from the village (family, friends, faith community, school, and neighbors) and lack of external control from the state (criminal justice system and system of laws and rules). Some blame social factors of environment, lack of parenting, peer pressure, poverty, lack of education, deteriorated neighborhoods. Some blame heredity and poor diet and nutrition, drug abuse, so-called crack babies, or alcohol-infused babies. Some blame crime victims for creating opportunity and motives for crime by victims hanging out in bars, with prostitutes, buying drugs, provoking the crime by their actions, and by not avoiding crime-ridden areas. Some believe that crime occurs because of self-interest, or narcissism, by trying to get the American dream quickly with a crime shortcut rather than working and saving for it in a low paying job. I do not know the cause of crime and am not sure there is only one. I do know that to commit a crime one has to first make the choice to do it. With that choice there had to be some level of a conscious assessment of the risk of getting caught and punished and feeling shame, regret and guilt.

When the offender is caught for the first time I think we need to look at how we treat him or her with the least severe sanction possible in the hopes it will not start the labeling and stigmatizing process. For minor crimes and for first time offenders as juveniles I see a possibility of family group conferencing as a diversionary alternative to incarceration. It may actually "save" a few from starting on the road to becoming a career criminal.

To me the kind of victim-offender mediation and family group conferencing described above in the vandalized church example is the restorative justice approach in a nutshell. I do want to make one thing clear: the victims here would not be forced in any way to take the restorative approach. They have the right to decline and let the state try the boy and give him two years probation if they so choose. The restorative justice approach only works when it is freely chosen by both parties in my opinion. Even though it has elements of a communitarian approach, it also retains rights and liberties that are demanded by civil libertarians and liberals. What if the boy had been a Satanist and the church wanted nothing to do with meeting him and wanted to allow the state to prosecute him? What if the boy had not wanted to meet with the church people and wanted to undergo traditional prosecution? That is his right as well. Both parties have the option.

The next time I have a criminal or civil case against someone I plan to see if there is a restorative justice victim offender mediator who could allow me and the offender to work it out before going into the adversarial court route. The reason is that I get more out of direct, mediated contact with the offender that way and I might even get more restitution and community service that way. I also get more respect from the offender and the criminal justice system than if I were a marginalized crime victim who only participated as a called witness or to make a victim impact statement after the conviction in the court. I do not think this kind of mediation is for every crime or for every crime victim. It probably would be for a small percentage of cases especially non-violent juvenile and adult cases. I would suspect that in cases of murder, rape, aggravated assault, child molestation, aggravated stalking, kidnapping it would be much less used or desired. It may even be counter-productive.

I would like to give one more example different from church breaking and entering but it is still a breaking and entering crime. In 1986 our home was burglarized and the offender was never found. If found and arrested and in jail, I fantasized that I would like to arrange a meeting in the jail on visiting day with the burglar, and his family and my family present along with a mediator. I wanted to all sit in a circle and go around the circle and discuss how the burglary made me and my wife angry and upset that the sanctity of our home had been violated. I would have told him how upset I was that he even took things worthless to him but meant the world to me that my grandmother had given to me before she died. I wanted to know what he did with the things he stole and whether he could get them back for me. I wanted a court order of restitution to compensate for the value of stolen items. I wanted him to do community service. If he had a drug problem, I wanted him to get help and drop random urines to make sure he wasn't using drugs again. I wanted to speak regularly with the offender in monitored and mediated sessions so we could develop and repair a broken relationship. I wanted to enlist his family in support of his getting better so he would not feel the need to resort to crime.

I wanted to pray for him and with him when we were in session if he would agree to it and the mediator would allow it. I wanted him to put things right again by allowing me to vent my disgust and anger over time. I wanted to see if I could work on the forgiveness process with the offender but I first needed to see some genuine (not lip service) remorse and acceptance of responsibility on his part. I wanted to work toward forgiveness if he would try to make amends with restitution and community service and attendance at mediated sessions. With no offender ever being caught in the burglary of my home I had to forgive the burglar in absentia and without the benefit of any of the above.

For burglaries, thefts, frauds, forgeries, minor assaults by juvenile or adult offenders I think restorative justice has a real possibility for breaking the cycle of arrest, trial, imprisonment and release and within a few years it starts all over. I do **not** think restorative justice works for drug offenses, most domestic violence cases and do not think it works in cases of extreme violence (I could be wrong here as I know they have tried it with cases of murder and rape but I would like to see the real statistics before I change my mind on this) In drug offenses the society at large is the victim. In stalking and domestic violence cases it puts the harmer close to the victim again and next time he may kill her. In cases of murder I just don't see it. I am open to the exceptional cases in which murderers sit down with surviving family members and healing occurs. I need to be convinced about restorative justice with murderers and I need to know what benefit or angle the inmate played before I change my mind.

Murder strikes at your heart and soul and is such a deep wound. I cannot see how meeting with the murderer in prison in a mediated session would "restore" the loss of the loved one, or lead to a restorative process other than getting a few questions answered, like why he says he did the crime. This "answer" as to why he did the crime will be a carefully crafted response and not necessarily the truth at all when appeals are still underway because it may jeopardize his appeal.

I have worked with enough murderers to know if they agreed to the mediated session I would want to know their angle first. I watched a show on *48 hours* where a mother talked to the murderer of her daughter in a Texas prison with the benefit of a psychologist who set the meeting up. The prisoner was on death row and promised in writing not to use any means of this talk with the crime victim to benefit his case for clemency, appeal, or leniency. Then I found out he wanted to donate his organs. In Texas they won't allow donated organs from executed inmates. To me it was a back door attempt to get his sentence commuted to life, so he could donate his organs and he used the TV forum to air his request. No one on the TV show saw this for what it was.

I think in cases of murder that restorative justice needs to be carefully evaluated. Victim-offender mediation could also re-traumatize the crime victim so much it could cause nightmares and rage all over again. In fact, just walking into a prison for the first time is scary but then adding the additional stress of facing the murderer of your loved one is almost too much. A video on how the victim (in cases of rape or murder) feels could be shown to the offender instead. In cases of rape it seems a good idea to show rape victims on video to rapists in prison rather than allow rape victims to come in person in order to avoid rapists vicariously being satisfied by the power trip of watching victims cry. It also avoids re-traumatization of the rape victims.

In my opinion, restorative justice is best served when the meeting is in the community of shalom, rather than in a prison or jail. Shalom, or peace, is the goal to be restored after the crime disturbed it. If all parties (victims and their supporters, offenders and supporters and the community) work toward restoring as much peace as is possible after the crime then the outcome will be more healing and less retributive in most cases.

Chapter 7

THE NEED FOR SUPPORT GROUPS FOR VICTIMS OF CRIME

Any ministry for crime victims needs to include pastoral care for those crime victims that are hurting, and wounded, both physically and spiritually. There are a lot of secular therapeutic programs that crime victims can use (psychiatrists, psychologists, social workers, licensed professional counselors, marriage and family therapists, as well as secular support groups). Pastoral care seeks to introduce prayer, scripture, caring structures, coping skills to overcome stress that naturally is caused by a horrible murder in the family.(note: Federal funds cannot support prayer and scripture activities and they must be separated in time/space from the funded program)

A pastoral care support group model should try to repair broken relational ties with the faith community, family and friends. This broken-ness is often experienced as a crisis of faith and a loss of trust in society when a homicide survivor sees how evil and hateful the murderer can be. Pastoral care models of criminal justice ministry have been directed in the past to prison ministry and law enforcement chaplaincy. CVAC is one of the few ministries in North America that includes pastoral individual sessions, family sessions, support groups by crime type (homicide, stalking, innocent parents of the abused child).

Other support groups for domestic violence, sexual assault, child abuse, elder abuse, assault and battery, robbery, theft, fraud, can just as easily be included or developed for crime victims. The support group movement is large in this country, the most notable being Alcoholics Anonymous, Rainbows and Compassionate Friends.

CVAC offers a homicide surviving family member an opportunity to meet weekly in a church and pray together, share the truth about the murder, give and receive help from persons who experienced a similar crime, facilitate coping skills for the stress-related trauma that the crime caused. The group promises to keep the matters discussed as confidential and although no one is forced to participate it is hoped that they will interact, rather than be silent. The circle prayer at the end is completely voluntary and members may pass without criticism.

The sharing and caring in the support group is deep because of the intensity of emotions. Oftentimes, severe crying occurs because of the feeling of loss and grief. Anger is expressed and listened to without judgment in order for ventilation and catharsis to occur. In addition to anger, grief, members express depression, confusion, and frustration as symptoms of the acute stress or post-traumatic stress reaction. Group members have stated they feel like they are losing their mind and "going crazy." They cannot work at all or they work like workaholics. They sleep too much or not at all. They overeat or do not feel like eating. They are irritable and snap at friends' family and coworkers or withdraw in isolation. They are hyper-vigilant, or hyper-aroused and easily startled. They are dysfunctional and have short term memory loss. They are obsessed with details of the crime. They complain of physical illness, soreness in body parts related to the grief and stress and often over medicate or self-medicate with drugs or alcohol to mute the intensity of the pain. Many of these symptoms occur because the trauma induced more stress in their lives than they are accustomed to handle.

The members ask questions about God, forgiveness, justice as divine and secular, the problem of evil, and all wonder why and how such a horrible evil act as the murder of their loved one could be allowed to happen. "Oh, God," or "Oh, my God," is a common expression exhibited by crime victims when they hear the news of the murder. Very soon after the murder a homicide family member of the deceased will offer a prayer to God to please not let this murder be true. Many group members want to know why God "allowed" this murder to occur.

The issue of the problem of evil and theodicy is often discussed in support groups which CVAC sponsors for homicide survivors. One particular homicide survivor group struggled with this problem and decided that God did not intend this murder because God intends good or Shalom (peace) for His people. An evil person disobeyed the will of God and His commandments to love Him and one another as oneself. The evil person chose to kill another because the evil in him or her led to the murder. The evil person broke the Shalom that God intended (in secular term he or she "disturbed the peace"). The vertical relationships between humans and God were broken by the murderous act. The evil person broke the Golden Rule to do unto others as you would have them do unto you. This murderous event broke the horizontal relationships of respect and love and standards of decency and care. The loving relationships and decency standards were altered by the effects of hatred, evil, deceit promulgated by the murderer or assaulter.

The nature of a self-help support group is to heal and "get better instead of bitter." A pastoral care support group calls upon spiritual resources to restore the person to as near wholeness and sanity as is possible. One cannot be made whole again as if the crime never happened, or as if the loved one could ever be replaced, but degrees of wholeness are possible with the care and support of faith, friends, family and sharing in a support group. The support group becomes a spiritual family of bonding, fellowship, closeness and may be "the church" for those who do not have a church, are agnostic or atheist, or do not have family or friends in the area.

Oftentimes, members of the support group call each other or meet during the week at lunch or dinner to talk further. The sharing in and out of group allows members to ventilate and get some catharsis. The "talking it out and talking it through" diminishes the power the offence has over their lives. With each retelling of the murder when a new member arrives, the group members experience a "desensitizing" to the horrific nature of the crime. Each time it gets a little easier to discuss it especially when discussing it has been discouraged or denied by friends and family who want the person to "get over it and get on with life." The sharing and caring support group is a listening post for someone who needs to tell their story to people with similar experiences.

A pastoral care model for the support group should include an evaluation component in order to provide feedback to the group members, and to determine if it is being effective at what it is attempting to do. Because one of the goals is to restore broken relationships on the horizontal, or personal, level and on the vertical or divine level a focus group evaluation model should address some of these questions. In one such focus group evaluation in January 2001 the members said they "felt encouraged by each other and no longer felt they were alone or crazy." They like both "getting and giving help because by helping others they moved beyond their own situation." They liked the mutual sharing and support because it was confidential. They could tell the truth among crime victims who had experienced a murder. They liked the nonjudgmental nature of the group and most liked the prayer as "soothing and healing." A member said it meant a lot to her and helped her when she heard others praying for her in the group. The group did not like religion but did like the spirituality of the group. One said she was angry at God at first but now finds the prayers soothing to her. An atheist member was irritated at first by the prayer but now thinks it is nice to be thought of by others.

The focus group evaluation revealed that the group members liked resources given out, liked being shown how to write a victim impact statement, file a victim compensation form, request victim notification of an offender's release, make a Freedom of Information Act or Open Records Act request, how to cope with the crime by talking of feelings to others, how to use Internet websites as resources, suggested books and articles. The group liked the "go-around" technique and helping the neediest first, use of role plays, counseling and listening skills (Rogerian client-centered). The group learned how to relax by using anger release techniques, meditation, exercise, and used physician-prescribed medication. Several group members expressed that they were unable to and learned by group members.

Another goal for the group is to learn coping skills for the stress experienced by the trauma of hearing about the murder and its aftermath. A support group model can use some techniques, like client-centered listening, psychodrama, guided interaction, relaxation exercises, but at the heart of all that is said or done there has to be caring and understanding. The leader of the group has to be honest and a participant. He or she should guide and facilitate the participants to ask for help and to help each other. The leader needs to listen deeply to hear what is being said beneath the words and draw the feelings out. He or she needs to facilitate discussion and interaction that enables the group to help each other through the problems, which is empowering. By helping others one can get beyond their own "sticking points." Basic education about the criminal justice system and describing victims' rights are important and should be accurate, but the group should be more than just that.

Real and genuine care for each other in the group is the most healing agent there is. The sharing of deep feelings of grief and anger and deep depression can be therapeutic and healing, but also can be clinically dangerous if someone becomes violent or suicidal. A trained leader can spot these violent or suicidal signs and make referrals.

Two techniques will be described in detail, the "talking stick" and the relaxation exercise. After the leader, or co-facilitator, opens with prayer the group begins with a relaxation exercise. The relaxation exercise is as follows: Imagine you are a tall glass of water and it will run down your spine through your toes. Take three deep breaths first. Breathe deeply in and reach a higher lobe of the lung than normal. Sit straight with eyes closed and hands on knees and now imagine the water is trickling down to behind your eyes. As it goes behind your eyes, relax your eyelids. Let the water run down to your throat, your chest and as it reaches your chest relax your shoulders. Let it run down to your stomach and to your hips, separating into right and left hips, turning down to the knees and then turning down to the ankles and then turning out to the toes and then out your toes completely leaving your body. One minute of silence. Now come back to where, you are and open your eyes. Share reactions briefly." That is one of the oft-used relaxation exercises.

The "talking stick" involves the use of a sacred object, like a Bible, a cross, a stone or piece of clothing from a deceased loved one. Then a common question is asked in sequence and each person holds the object while talking. No one else talks or asks questions but tries to "deeply listen, or hear the meaning behind the words." After all have talked a form of respectful questions or statements can be made to each other. The motive for the reflection and questions should be healing in nature, to "build another up" rather than "put a person down." Some people may talk with the object in hand for as long as 10 minutes and others may be brief and conclude in a few minutes.

To measure the coping skills the leader can use an online test found at www.PsychTests.com, called Coping Skills Inventory Test that is a 45 question test that can be taken in 20 minutes and scored online for a small fee. It measures seven variables, such as reactivity to stress, ability to assess situations, self-reliance, resourcefulness, adaptability, proactive attitude, and the ability to relax.

During a six months period from September 2000 to March 2001 there were 19 Coping Skills Inventory Tests given to homicide survivors by the Chaplain. During that time frame there were 20 homicide survivor support group sessions held weekly for 1.5 hours and 96 attendees (average of 4.8 per session). Some groups were canceled for holidays or bad weather. A core group of eight attended five or more times and 12 others came less than five times. Four persons attended 14, 14, 13 and 11 times each. Eight of the Homicide support group took the pre-test and the post-test. Their mean score was 66.375 and their average post-test score was 73.63; t of -3.55; and p of <.01. The mean improvement in coping skills was about seven points. All post test scores improved and none went down. Only two of the stalking victims took the pre and post test and both went up five points and four points respectively. Nine others took the pretest but did not take the post test as they moved or came too infrequently.

The number studied is too small and time frame too short to make any generalizations about the effectiveness of a support group for surviving family members of a homicide but it does bear further research to determine if preliminary positive findings can be replicated. Two factors make the test noteworthy: the test is immediately scored on the Internet and it costs very little. Other tests may be good but they take time and a lot of money to score. The test does measure coping skills which is a goal of the group but complete reliance on the test by itself is not recommended. There are at least 18 other tests in the counseling profession that measure coping skills as well and other useful tests on depression, anxiety and anger. The focus group evaluation is just as important and revealing about the group's sense of healing and improvement. It is recommended that coping skills testing and focus group models should be used together for evaluation purposes.

Chapter 8

SURVIVOR STORIES

My son Jeffrey

My name is Holly Phillips

On December 23, 2001, my sons, Jeffrey and Brandon, were both home and excited about Christmas. Jeffrey, 19, was watching a movie with a young lady named Angela, whom he had been dating off and on for a year. Brandon, 15, was on the phone with his girlfriend. It was about 11:00 p.m. My husband, Tony, and I decided we would go on to bed. Everyone was here safe and happy. At about 11:30 p.m. Brandon came into our room, woke us, and said that there was a lady on the phone about Jeffrey. He had been in an accident. I was so confused. I did not understand as we all got dressed. I was praying to God, please let him be okay. I was thinking he was in a car wreck. I could not understand because he was just here in his home safe. When we got to the old Winn-Dixie shopping center there were two ambulances, police cars, and his friends standing all around. His friends were crying. I was crying, screaming at them, "What happened?" I was trying to get to my son, but no one would let me. I saw him crying and struggling on the cold hard pavement. I was yelling to him, "I love you Jeffery, Momma's here." I grabbed one of his friends, Matt, and started yelling at him, "How could you let this happen to my baby? He was your friend."

The police came over and told us some of what had happened. They said two guys had jumped Jeffrey and beat him with bats. They said they were waiting for the life helicopter to take him to Grady Trauma Center. They assured me he was going to be okay. They said for us to go on to Grady as the helicopter got there and we could meet it there. I wanted to see Jeffrey but they said no. I didn't understand as we were reassured he was going to be okay. We were getting in our truck to go to Grady. One of the paramedics came up to me and gave me my son's jewelry. I thanked her and asked her to please tell Jeffrey that Momma loves him very much. As we rushed to Grady Hospital, I was praying the entire time. Please God, let my son be okay. He is such a fine young man. When we got to Grady, we asked the information clerk about our son, Jeffrey. She told us that they decided to take him to Kennestone, which was only four miles from our home. She told us that this was a good sign so we rushed back to Kennestone. As we were walking to the walkway, I saw about 20 of Jeffrey's friends crying and screaming. I knew then he had died. I dropped to my knees and started crying and screaming.

I don't remember much after that until Christmas morning, when my home was filled with family and friends. As I watched everyone open their presents, I was so sad thinking my son should be here to see all the surprises I bought for his Explorer. They handed me a gift that Jeffrey bought me for Christmas. As I opened it up, it was a white teddy bear with a blue ribbon. He named it Frosty. I pressed its paw and it said "I love you." I started crying and so did everyone in the room. I ran to my bedroom and cried uncontrollably. My son, Brandon, came and sat in my lap. We cried together for a long time.

December 27, 2001 was my son Jeffrey's funeral. There were more than 350 people in attendance I was told. The Cobb County police department and SWAT team gave us a police escort like one of their own had died. Every light and intersection was blocked. I don't remember much when we got to the church. I looked at a crowd of family and friends but recognized none. They led me to the front where my son's Dolphin urn was. People had put flowers, gifts and a small dirt bike around his urn. Then several of his friends stood up and said a speech about Jeffrey. He was well loved and they had all looked up to him as the leader of strength and goodness. They knew he was the logical one and wanted to do right by God and his family in life.

After the funeral I was numb for months. My mind knows he is still alive and that he is on a long needed vacation. My heart and soul have been ripped in two. I have so much hatred in my heart, for Jeffrey had been called by two of his friends on December 23, 2001 to ask him to help them. They were being beat up and chased all over Marietta. They wanted to come to our home. Jeffrey told them no. He would meet them at the Winn-Dixie. Jeffrey went as the peacemaker. When he got there, all the boys were arguing. Jeffrey got them to settle down and talk everything over and they reached an agreement. However, in the middle of the argument Jay Body and Joey Holt called Daryl Burton and Josh Thompson. He told them they needed to come help them take care of this big guy they could not handle. But they never called them back to tell them the argument was over. As everyone was getting in their cars to go home, my son Jeffrey was walking back to his car where he parked it out of the way so it would not get damaged in case something happened. That was when Daryl, Josh and Chris drove up. Daryl and Josh jumped out of their truck and went after my son. They did not even know him. Daryl got in front of Jeffrey and Josh got behind him. Daryl pushed Jeffrey and Josh grabbed my son's bat from behind and they took turns beating him with it. As my son was running for his life they did not stop hitting him and no one came to his rescue. As he lay on the ground, he begged them to stop, crying and saying, "I'm sorry." They did not care and continued beating him. Finally, Josh took the bat and ran up to Jeffrey's friend's car and asked if they wanted the same and then jumped back into his truck and took off.

Daryl Burton had just been released from jail on December 14, 2001 and Josh Thompson on December 7, 2001, both released to their parents. Daryl was on intensive probation. The justice system and the boys' parents did not give a damn about these two thugs. They were allowed to do what they wanted and this is reason my son is not with us today. I have not dealt with this very well at all. I'm depressed every single day, and I cry all the time. There is a huge hole in my heart. I kiss Jeffrey's urn and picture every morning and night. I know he is in a better place but my heart still hurts. I am fortunate to have my other son, Brandon whom I love just as much, and my husband, Tony. They are my strength now. When I cry, they hold me and share my pain. I could not go on without them.

I talk with Jeffrey and play our song, *Tell My Why* almost every day. I have nightmares all the time. I feel every day I become more depressed. I have now had to learn how to cook for three instead of four. I have a hard time with holidays, and there is such an empty feeling here. I had to face Mother's Day without his teddy bear hugs and kisses telling me he loved me and the surprises he would give. He was always doing special things for me. He would bring me roses just to say "I love you, Mom" and thanks for everything you do for me. He would leave me notes telling me he loves me. I had to face his 20th birthday without him. All his friends came over with flowers, cards and gifts. We sang "Happy Birthday" to him and Brandon blew out the candle. We went to the parking lot where he died and placed flowers and notes on his pole. We released 20 balloons that we all signed and 20 note cards attached. We said a prayer and played our song. Everyone cried and hugged each other.

On my good days I can smile and laugh. On my bad days all I do is cry. Every day is a new day without Jeffrey. I have a lonely place in my heart that cannot be replaced Brandon and Tony are the only reason I get up each day and want to live. I know I will never be able to see Jeffrey get married and give me grandchildren. I will always miss our nights sitting up and discussing his dreams, wants, future and the things that make him happy or sad. Now, I have only Brandon to watch get married and give me grandchildren. This is what is keeping me going and happy. I know Jeffrey is in heaven and watching over us. He is an angel. I know he is still in our home. He turns fans, opens and closes doors. This gives me comfort. I dream of him and he is always smiling at me.

Tony asked me if I would always be miserable. All I could say was I that I didn't know. I try very hard to keep my feelings to myself so no one can see my pain, they don't deserve it. I go to a support group led by Bruce Cook every Tuesday night. I always go in there with a heavy heart, but by the time I leave there is a weight off my shoulder that I cannot explain. This group has really helped my husband and me. I know that every breath I take and heartbeat that I feel, I am one step closer to being with my beloved son. I am not in any hurry, I have Brandon and Tony to take care of and watch other dreams come true. I pray every day for God to continue watching over us and taking care of us. I pray Jeffrey and my mother continue to watch over us and show me signs of their beautiful place and peace. I love you my precious son, Jeffrey. May stars forever shine on your behalf!

Love Mom, May 28, 2002

My son Stephen

My name is Julie Allen and I am a surviving victim of homicide.

On July 30, 1999, I received the most horrible news a mother could ever receive. My youngest son, Stephen Allen, was shot and killed. I will never forget that night when I got the phone call that he had been shot in the head by one of his friends. I have never been the same and will never be the same. I had heard all of my life that burying a child is the hardest thing you could ever do in your life. I speak from experience, believe me it is the truth. You see my daddy buried his son Clay, who was my half brother, in 1983. I saw how that murder changed his life. Because of the murder of my half brother, I was a very protective mother of my sons, Ricky and Stephen. I was very disappointed with our judicial system. The man that killed Clay was sentenced to life in prison and walked out in 7 and 1/2 years.

I divorced in 1989 and my life was my sons. I was everything to them, mother, daddy, doctor, teacher, etc., but most of all I was their friend. I worry about my oldest son Ricky. I feared that something will happen to him. If I don't talk to him every day, I don't think I could function, but I talked to him every day before Stephen's death. Stephen called me every day too. Sometimes I still sit and wait for the phone to ring to hear his voice say, "Hey Mom, what are you doing?"

This year it will be three years since I laid my baby to rest and it doesn't get any easier. The pain is still as strong now as it was then. I don't think it will ever go away. Some days are not as bad as others, but there is not a day that goes by that my heart does not ache. I miss him so much. I am still angry that Rodolfo Rodriquez took him from me. The courts dropped his murder sentence to involuntary manslaughter because they were friends and there was not a witness in the room where this tragedy took place. They gave him five years and this is very hard to handle too.

One day I received a letter from CVAC inviting me, family and friends to a Memorial in honor of victims of murder in February 2000 and I called the number and talked to Bruce Cook giving him Stephen's name to be put on a wall and to have his name read and a candle lit in his memory. After I gave Bruce the information, he asked me how I was doing and I lost it. I was hardly able to talk from crying. He told me that there was a support group that met every Tuesday night at Vinings Methodist Church at 7:30 and invited me to be a part of this group. If it wasn't for this group, I don't think I would be where I am today.

Finally (people, now friends) who actually knew how I felt have been the biggest part of my healing. This group and Bruce have helped more than any doctor or prescription. I thank God for them every day. A horrible crime like this changes you and your life, but you can't give up because then the murderer gets another victim. The only thing that eases my mind is that "eternal justice" will be served and I will see Stephen again one day.

Grandma's Precious Baby Sierra

My name is Joanne Thomas.

On May 3, 1999, my four-and-a-half-year old granddaughter, Sierra Beth Soto was playing on a day care center playground in Costa Mesa, California in Orange County when an evil offender intentionally drove his car through a chain link fence into the children killing Sierra and a three-year-old boy named Brandon. The offender injured seven other children and a teacher. When the car stopped against a tree, Sierra and Brandon were underneath the car. The offender just sat in the car. When the police arrived and asked him what happened, he said, "I wanted to execute the children because they are innocent."

That was the day my life changed forever. I loved Sierra more than anything else in this world. She taught me joy and real unconditional love. Sierra was born on September 15, 1994, and two weeks later I moved to California and helped take care of her. I was with her until October 4, 1996, when I moved back to Georgia. My whole life revolved around when I would get to see her or talk to her on the telephone.

She was an awesome little girl and everyone who came into contact with her loved her. She was my daughter Cindy's only child and my heart breaks for her. I wish I could take the pain away but I can't. Cindy owns a dance studio in California, and Sierra was born dancing. Oh, how she loved to dance.

I remember one time when the children from the dance studio performed at Disney land. I was sitting in front of the stage with Sierra in her stroller before the show started. There was music playing and she climbed out of her stroller and crawled up the steps to the stage. She stood up and started dancing. Everybody walking by started clapping and she loved it. It was as if she were saying "Hey, everyone watch me dance." She was such a little stage ham.

I remember the first time I went back to California to see her. Cindy and Sierra were standing at the foot of the ramp. When I started down the ramp Sierra saw me and broke away from Cindy and ran up the ramp to me. I dropped everything and grabbed her into my arms and turned round and round, stopping everyone from getting off the plane. I had never in my life felt such love. Her last two Christmases, Cindy and Sierra came to Georgia to spend Christmas with me. They would always arrive on Christmas day. I would decorate the tree but leave the lower branches for her to decorate when she got here.

Now at Christmas time when I decorate the tree, it breaks my heart when I get to the lower branches. Sierra's favorite color was purple so now my tree has purple bulbs and silver glitter bulbs and lots of angel ornaments. She loved glitter and always wanted glitter paint on her when she danced.

One day when I was visiting her, we were walking to the park and I looked down at her and said "You are grandma's precious baby," and she replied, "Grandma I am not a baby, I'm a big girl." I said, "Yes, you are a big girl." She thought for a moment and then she looked up at me and said, "I guess I can be your baby." When I think of that moment my heart fills with joy. There is not a day that goes by that I don't think of my precious baby and wonder why she had to be taken from us. When Sierra was murdered, I was so afraid that my daughter would sink into a deep depression but she didn't. She told me that she had decided that if she locked herself in a dark room that the man on trial for Sierra's death would win. Instead, she started Sierra's Light Foundation to set up guidelines for safety for day care centers and to help build walls around playgrounds to ensure the safety of the children.

Cindy has spoken at meetings of the California state legislature to try to get laws passed for child safety in all schools. She was able to get a new law passed in Costa Mesa, California in regard to playground safety for daycare centers and elementary schools. They will be using some of Sierra's Light Foundation safety guidelines.

I was very proud of her when she was presented with The Scars into the Stars Award by Dr. Robert Schuller at the Crystal Cathedral for all the work she had done for the protection of our children.

Nothing can bring Sierra back but if her work can save just one child it can give some comfort to her.

My daughter called me one day to tell me that a truck had gone out of control and hit one of the steel reinforced walls that Sierra's Light Foundation had built but no children were hurt in the incident because the concrete walls and the steel rods stopped it from going into the playground. A small plaque is put on each of the walls built, in memory of Sierra and Brandon.

When the trial started I knew I wanted the offender to die for what he did, but I also knew I did not want my daughter to have to relive Sierra's death for the next 20 years every time there is an appeal. The trial was horrible. Cindy was not allowed to show any emotion in the courtroom.

She was not even allowed to cry. It is so true that the criminals have all the rights and the victims and their families have no rights. Where was Sierra's right to live a full and happy life? The offender took that away from her.

The offender pleaded not guilty by reason of insanity. Thank goodness the jury did not buy that. This man had been in and out of hospitals and was supposed to be on medication. The last time he was in the hospital, a psychiatrist wanted to keep him and the hospital said no, so they released him. Just before he drove to the play ground, he had forced two cars off the road on the freeway. The people in one of the cars called the police on their cell phone but, it was too late to save the children as he was already driving down the street the daycare center was on. According to the people who witnessed the murder, the offender drove past the Center, then turned his car around and aimed it at the playground. I believe that this evil man murdered Sierra, but God was there to pick her up and take her to heaven. So many tiny little miracles have happened to let me know that she is still with me and the bond between us will never die.

I want to tell a few stories that are so real to me that I know without a doubt she is still with me in spirit. Sierra loved pinwheels, so I put a purple and silver pinwheel outside in a flower pot. That pinwheel will start turning even when there is no wind. One day my neighbor and I were walking from our cars to our apartment. As we were walking down the sidewalk, all of a sudden the pinwheel started turning faster and faster. My neighbor turned to me and said "Look at that pinwheel turning and there is no wind." I looked at her and smiled and said, "I know." She did not know about Sierra.

A few months after Sierra was killed I was sitting alone in my office and was crying and I kept saying to myself and to Sierra if only I could hug you one more time. About three minutes later, one of the doctors that I work for walked by my office and I heard her say, "Tell Miss Joanne hello." I looked up and there was a little girl about four years old with a big smile like Sierra's. She ran to me and put her arms around me and gave me a big hug. I felt Sierra so close to me at that moment. After she walked out of the room, I felt such a calm come over me and all I could feel was a "thank you to Sierra" for Grandma Joanne's hug.

A couple of days later I was in a Target store looking for something. There was a little girl about three or four year's old sitting in a shopping cart. She was with her mother. The little girl said the shoes that I was looking at were pretty. I looked at her and said "Yes they are," and I smiled at her. Then to my amazement she said, "Can I have a hug." I almost fell over. I looked at her mother and asked if it was okay to give the little girl a hug and she said yes.

Again, I felt Sierra so close. The last Christmas that I had with Sierra, I had bought her a music box doll at the San Francisco Music Box. The doll had pig tails. Cindy told me that when she would get upset with her mom she would go into her room and play her music box doll and say over and over "I want my grandma, Joanne." She always called me "Grandma Joanne." When Sierra was buried, Cindy put the music box doll in her casket with her.

Just before the sentencing of the offender, I happened to go into the San Francisco music box store and was looking around when I spotted a music box doll with dark hair, wearing a white lace dress. She was holding a little cross and a little bible. The song was *Jesus Loves Me*. For some reason, I had to have that doll. When I got home I wound it up and let it play until it stopped. I then put it on a shelf on which I keep some things of Sierra's. About two hours later my daughter called to tell me that the offender's sentence was life in prison without parole.

When I hung up the phone, I looked at Sierra's picture and said, "He can never hurt another child again, baby." Just as I said it the music box started playing. It was only for a few seconds and I knew that she had heard me.

Now for the story of the purple beads: Sierra's favorite color was purple and she loved to play with my beads. Not long after I'd come home from California (I was there a month after she died), I kept praying and asking for a sign so I would know that she was okay. This went on for a few days. One morning as I was going out the door to go to work, I looked down and there right in front of me was a strand of purple beads. That was my sign.

This past Christmas I was talking out loud to her and said "Grandma Joanne needs a Christmas present from you." I parked my car and when I got out I looked down and on the ground, there was a candy cane made out of purple beads. I know that some people would say that all this is in my head and it is wishful thinking. I choose to think if you believe that your loved ones are always with you and that their spirits will never go away and that love never dies. Because my daughter lives so far away and even though I talked to her three or four times a week it was difficult just living. I could not stop crying and I had to be put on medications. If it had not been for Bruce Cook of CVAC and all the people in the support group who had loved ones murdered, I would not have survived.

So many people say move on it's been long enough, and you need to get over it. They can never know (unless it has happened to them) just how devastating it is to lose someone you love through murder. You never get over it. Sometimes I think I am okay, and will trigger me and I am back to square one. Sometimes I think of the details—not that I want to but, it just comes into my head without warning. One of the worst things that happened was that I found out about a year later was that the police found Sierra's earring in one of the tires.

When I heard about another little girl five years later that was murdered in Orange County, California by a man who grabbed her, she was kicking and screaming to get away. They found her body and she was naked and had been raped and murdered. I can't imagine the terror that little girl felt. I thank God that Sierra did not know what hit her and that she died instantly. I feel so bad for that other little girl's parents and I pray to God that they can survive what happened to their beautiful little girl. The picture in the paper reminded m e so much of Sierra.

The same smile, eyes, and hair. My daughter called to ask me if I had seen the picture of the little girl who was killed. It reminded her of Sierra, too. I sometimes wonder how we have the strength to get through something like this and still are able to function! All I know is that God is always with me even when I am angry with him. He lets me be angry, He lets me cry. He brings me peace and lets me know that Sierra is always here with me. As Dr. Schuller said to my daughter when she asked him about some things that had happened to her that made her know that Sierra was still with her. He said, "All you have to have is love and have an open mind. Open to the beauty that you find in this world if you just look." I know that someday I will see Sierra again.

My Daughter Karen

My name is Gail Laney

July 10, 1998 was the day our 33 year-old daughter, Karen, was murdered. She had been tied up, gagged, brutally battered and bitten. The cause of death was strangulation. Her murderer was a helper on a moving van passing through our city that had stopped for the night, and four months later he was apprehended in another state. He was tried two years later, found guilty, and has been sentenced to life in prison.

Our devastation was greater than I could ever have imagined. My husband and I sank into deep depression. My every thought was of Karen and what she must have suffered. We performed ordinary duties, but withdrew from everyone and everything. Both of us developed high blood pressure, gained weight, began to suffer other physical problems, and experienced crying episodes. We sought help through counselors, psychologists and psychiatrists, but none were able to provide the help we needed. I began using anti-depressants in order to function, but when a year had passed and I was not able to cope any better than I had in the beginning, I became desperate. I felt that if I didn't get some help from somewhere, I would actually lose my mind.

It was at this point that we received a letter from the Crime Victims Advocacy Council (CVAC) that provided information about weekly meetings for homicide victims. I met people who had lost family members in much the same way as I had—people who had experienced the same emotions and the same anger as I was feeling. Those of us in the group were able to share our pain with others who understood. My feelings of isolation began to disappear. I began to learn ways of coping with my tragedy, and soon realized that grief such as mine, under my set of circumstances, is perfectly normal. Being able to talk about Karen and the way she had died and to express my anger openly was the greatest healer of all. No one was judgmental and everyone was supportive. I began to learn about the justice system, how it works, and my legal rights as a victim.

We lived through numerous trial dates waiting for our daughter's murderer to be tried, only to be disappointed again and again each time until the trial was continued. Our grieving process was put on hold while the judicial system slowly worked its way to our case. After the second anniversary of Karen's death, we made an appointment with the District Attorney and pleaded that he try this criminal so that we could at least move toward another phase of our lives. When the time for trial finally arrived, members of CVAC were in the courtroom with us and rejoiced with us as the verdict was read. The fourth anniversary of Karen's death is approaching and I still think of her constantly. The whole structure of our family has changed. Karen's little girl is now seven years old and lives with her father. We have not seen Emma for three and a half years, something that never would have happened had Karen been alive, and we grieve for that loss. Karen's son, Nicolas, lives with our other daughter in another state. Nicolas' father was killed in an automobile accident when Nicolas was a baby, so he has been left with no parent and has only recently been allowed to have contact with his little sister.

The passage of time has eased our suffering, but the help of CVAC was my turning point. My prayer now is that God will use my loss and what I have learned to help others in need so that my daughter's death will not be in vain.

My Great-Nephew Little John Ramsey

My Niece-in-law Robyn and my Nephew

This is my story, April Shaw.

On September 22, 1997, it took one phone call to change my whole life. My older sister called from Indianapolis telling me my nephew, John (her only son) had murdered his wife, Robyn and their six-month old son, Little John. It seems murder was the farthest thing from the police's mind as they searched John's house. They had come there to arrest him on charges of armed robbery of a string of Pizza Huts. He evidently knew they were on to him, so he went on the run. When the police went to the house to serve a warrant, his roommate allowed them in to search the house. Instead of the robbery money they were searching for, to their horror they found the bodies of his wife and child, Robyn and Little John, stuffed in a freezer stored in the garage. For over six months, he had kept them frozen until he could find a place to bury them.

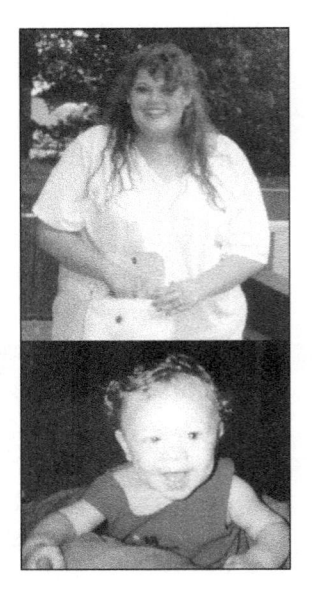

I will never forget how incomprehensible what my sister was telling me what had happened. It was so unbelievable that I actually hung up and called my aunt in Indianapolis and asked her had she heard anything on the news. When she confirmed that it had been flashing over breaking news, it was even on CNN, I still did not want to believe this was happening. More terribly, I couldn't believe I now had to go next door to tell my mother that her first born grandson murdered a granddaughter-in-law she adored and a great-grandson she would never have a chance to hold or kiss. Then I knew as the strong one in the family I would have to board a plane and fly to Indianapolis to deal with this tragedy. I don't remember after that night when I was able to sleep or eat again. This began the infamous "a foot in my stomach" feeling that I still get every now and then, even three years later.

I never had an opportunity to meet Robyn because I lived in Atlanta. But I had heard wonderful things about her—most notably her love for John and her son. She loved children and was a good mother. My family fell in love with her. When she had Little John, my family was so happy for her and John. John had a rough life, where we suspect he had been abused by my sister. So it was so good to hear that he was what we were led to believe, to be getting his life together. He seemed to have broken off ties from his mother and seemed to be happy to find someone to truly love him.

What triggered him to begin robbing Pizza Huts and then to murder his family we may never know. He doesn't seem to know himself, or he is reluctant to say why. He is now being evaluated to see if he is competent to stand trial, since the state is seeking the death sentence. He wants to die, so he is saying very little that will help his case or provide explanation.

Having a loved one commit such a horrendous crime produces many mixed emotions. It is so hard to believe that this little boy who used to call me mommy and loved for me to tickle him, would grow up to murder his own wife and child. If this had been anyone else, I would have said this person is a monster and society should get rid of him. How do you deal with loving a monster? It can be so confusing to continue to love that little boy but at the same time wanting the monster to pay for what he did. At first I felt so ashamed to have a family member who has murdered his family. Amazingly, people have been so supportive and understanding. But it still didn't help with my conflicting and confusing feelings. This was eating me up inside. Then I felt so bad for Robyn, I had an aching urge to apologize for what my nephew had done to her. It really hurts to know that I will never get the opportunity to hold and tickle my great-nephew, the way I did his father. There was so much to cry for and to cry over. I found I had to cry all the way to work so I would be able to work once I arrived.

I knew I needed to find a support group or some grief counseling. This was eating me up and I couldn't go to my family for I needed to be strong for them. I sought a support group and I believe God led me to CVAC. I had been referred to a few organizations but CVAC was the only one that returned my call. I knew I needed a spiritually-based organization and a group that would understand the turmoil I was feeling. I didn't want to have to explain this depth of grief and I didn't want to feel like an odd-ball. I needed the support of others who would understand my pain, confusion, and anger. See, unlike other grief, some closure comes with the finality of the funeral but with homicide the closure may not come for years.

Once you bury your loved ones, the next step is to deal with bringing the responsible parties to justice. And, an even greater trial is to live with a family member murdering another family member. In my case, there will never be any closure either, because my nephew's case is going to go on for years, since it is a death penalty case. If and when the legalities are worked through, he will either be imprisoned for life in prison or a mental institution, or my family will have to deal with another death when he is put to death.

For now, my healing comes in knowing I buried Robyn with her baby boy, Little John, by a nice shaded tree next to a school yard, where the sounds of children can be heard all day. And, when I need them my friends from CVAC are always there to help me through the rough times.

Billy Joe Kilgore: Father of Rhonda Kastl

Marie L. Richards: Sister of Kellie Wiggins

Double Homicide

Billy Joe and Marie were long time friends. But neither of them knew very much about "JJ." He was dropped off at Billy Joe's house on a warm Friday morning on May 21, 2004. JJ wanted to earn some extra money by washing cars and doing odd jobs around Billy Joe's house. He knew JJ's mother and allowed him to work. Later in the day, the two went together to run some errands including making a stop by the bank to cash a check. JJ stayed in the car at the bank, but knew Billy Joe had cashed a check. They arrived back at Billy Joe's house to get a part for his pool. JJ waited in the car. In the meantime, Marie stopped by to visit Billy Joe, he explained that he was about to leave and offered for anyone to go along. Marie said she would go along, not knowing that JJ is in the car. Having never met him, they are introduced and he moves to the back seat. What happened next? We will never know the truth of the story. We will never know the "Why." We do not know why or how JJ was able to get Billy Joe to pull over in a vacant lot covered in kudzu. We do not know how JJ was able to get Billy Joe's personal gun from his home. We do not know how they struggled for the gun. We do know they were robbed & murdered. Both Billy Joe & Marie were shot in the car. JJ could see that the first shot to Marie did not kill her, so he fired a second shot to her head, ensuring her death.

    The next day two boys passed by the vacant lot and saw something that looked like a car down in a ravine. As they approach to get a closer look, they found Billy Joe face down, pockets turned inside out and brutally murdered. It wasn't until police arrived that they found Marie dragged under brush and trash also viciously murdered. Apparently after JJ shot them he tried to steal the car & had removed their bodies. JJ had fled the scene with Marie's purse and the gun inside. He was arrested 3 days later on Monday afternoon in North Carolina with his girlfriend.

Rhonda & Kellie had never met until a year later at the first hearing for the trial. They instantly bonded and talked for hours on the phone comparing their story of how they found out about the murders and discovering more about Billy Joe & Marie. Their families needed each other to endure 3 and half years of hearings leading up to the Nov 26, 2007 trial date. The District Attorney sought the death penalty for both victims. JJ was found guilty on all three counts; 2 counts of murder and one for armed robbery for Marie. Both Kellie and Rhonda had received help from CVAC in preparing their Victim Impact Statements and during the penalty phase they each read a gripping statement of how this murder has affected their lives and the lives of their families.

Victory & Justice was received for Marie & Billy Joe and JJ was sentenced to the death penalty on December 13, 2007.

Both Rhonda & Kellie have separate portions to discuss about their personal involvement in CVAC and the support group.

Rhonda Kastl's portion on CVAC

I was very fortunate to find the CVAC support group a few months after my dad had been murdered. I remember being so afraid and uncomfortable attending my first time. I was afraid that everyone in the group would think that I was crazy or a horrible person for having the feelings that I had at the time. There are many stages that you go through being a homicide victim. I was in the angry stage when I first joined the group. I was actually afraid to speak a word other than to tell "my story." I was afraid to share my anger and my feelings of grief with the others. I soon realized that I was not alone. I realized that I was not crazy and that I was not a horrible person for feeling the emotions that I felt. The words that other members of the group were speaking were my words. Those were the same exact feelings and thoughts that I was experiencing. They helped me understand that what I was going through was all normal and that it was okay to feel that way. I realized that I was just like them.

We all shared one common denominator...we had lost someone that we love to an act of senseless violence. We shared the same feelings, emotions, grief, hurt, pain and anger. We all had a story to tell, each one being very different but we shared the same feelings. I remember going in thinking that no one else could be feeling what I was feeling; no one is going to understand what I am going through. I heard the story of one woman who had lost her child to a violent murder and she was also attacked but she survived. I looked at her and I thought to myself, if she can survive what she went through with losing her daughter and being attacked and here she is now helping me and others, then I can move forward one day too. She motivated me into not going into the deep depression that I was headed for. I was in awe of her story of survival, which gave me hope. I then became more comfortable and I attended the weekly meetings for almost 2 years. They understood and had compassion for me that no one else did. Not even my family or closest friends could understand what was really going on inside of me. I had friends during this time that simply could not understand or deal with my pain. They slowly drifted away from me. I found people in the support group who ended up being more supportive to me than those that I just thought were my friends. The members of the support group were able to understand me like no one else could. We could cry together; we laughed together; we shared each other's family triumphs and tragedy. We all had a special bond that could not be found anywhere else.

A year or so later I came back to the group and brought Kellie with me, the sister of the victim that was killed with my dad. We were able to talk and share with each other what we were going through and share our stories of my dad and her sister who were friends. We developed a friendship and were also able to give support to each other. I do not think I could have dealt with a death penalty trial if I had not had Kellie and her family there with us for support. Two families who did not know each other were drawn together and supported each other in a time of tragedy for us both. Her family along with my family was all suffering in so much pain and grief, but yet we were able to be there for each other. When we were getting prepared to attend the death penalty trial against the person who killed our family members, CVAC was very helpful in explaining to us the judicial system and gave us much needed insight as to what to expect during the trial. We were given advice on how to prepare our victim's impact statements. We shared statements with other members of the group who had already been through the process that we were about to go through. We learned so much from the other members who had already been through the trial process. They gave us insight as to what to expect during the trial.

I really do not know where I would be right now or how I could have coped without the support of CVAC. I wish everyone who had the misfortune of losing a loved one to homicide had the support of CVAC that I had.

Kellie Wiggins Portion on CVAC

Is she dead?

That is the question that has changed our lives forever. As the officer hesitated, my heart could see the truth in his eyes, although my mind wanted to comprehend otherwise.

Pounding and pounding the floor, clawing at the floor boards trying to deny the hellish void that was overtaking me, screaming and screaming in utter disbelief, pounding and pounding beating and clawing at the floor. . . my face slowly sliding in tears across the floor in total and utter devastation while trying to process, if I myself, was about to die. I caught a glimpse of my mother falling out of the chair as she was trying to grasp the news of Marie. I feared she was going into cardiac arrest from the sheer shock of the news of her daughter.

It is not possible to place into words on paper that describe gruesome murder, unspeakable wickedness, evil and fathom events so horrifying you cannot possibly process them and remain sane. Words fail me when trying to explain the emptiness and emotions of knowing they are never coming home again. Life as I know it is no more. JJ has forever changed that.

The details of what has been described previously about Marie & Billy Joe is only a slight sketch of the massive events and details that go into any murder and death penalty trial. Their deaths have tested my faith. It has taken me to very core of what I have always said I believe about God. My faith has literally been on trial. I knew that I was engaged in a spiritual battle and I needed all the help I could get. I had feelings of this huge void in my life. It had always been me and my sister and I was not prepared to be an only child to my mother. Marie was only 36 when she was murdered and I felt cheated of our lives together as sisters. At the time my children were 6 and 3, and they really helped keep my mind occupied and I had to move forward for them and my husband. A few months after Marie's murder "Greif Share" was offered at our church and my mother and I attended this together for 13 weeks. It was very timely and very much needed. However, we were the only ones in class that were dealing with a homicide and that is very different from other kinds of death. There was a friend in the class whose brother had recently committed suicide and although we grieved together we could not understand the vast difference of taking one's own life and one taking the life another. She seemed to have more closure. It was over; the person responsible for her brother's death was him and he was dead. I knew I had years looming ahead of me and I would be facing a judicial system I knew nothing about. My mother coped better than I had expected her to. We both have a very deep faith and a strong church family with a caring pastor and wife that have helped us a lot. I began to read all kinds of books that I thought would help me move forward in understanding how this could have happened to my sister and how I was going to deal with it. I tried to stay current on my Bible study and I began noting verses that I felt related to the trial. I compiled a binder of these verses and prayed them and read them over and over. They were specific to me and what was relevant to me at the time. I read books from Charles Stanley about adversity and spiritual warfare, authors like Nancy Grace, Max Lucado, and even Sharon Rocha's story about her daughter Laci Peterson. Probably the book that helped me the most was Ray Pritchard's book "Stealth Attack: Satan's Plan to destroy your life".

As we moved closer to the trial date I felt unprepared in presenting a Victim Impact Statement. Rhonda had encouraged me to attend the support group with CVAC and gain some help in preparing my statement. Other than Rhonda and my mother I had not been around other people affected by homicide and I was emotionally stripped as I sat in the group and faced my true feeling about what had happened to Marie. As I began to explain to Dr. Bruce Cook my version of what happened to Marie I realized I was telling someone for the first time in my own words what happened, that had not known Marie or what happened to her from my perspective. I listened to others speak their pain. I heard them use words and phrases that I could relate to and understand and felt. I was also being heard by people who really knew the depths of my battle and acknowledged that what I was saying was true and very real. I could see the pain gouged in their hearts and the hollowness of their eyes as they tried their best to find the words to express anger, confusion, depression, hatred, heartache and desperation. Sometimes words would not come and the blank stares on the floor are all that could be seen. Dr. Bruce would tell us to get it out and not hold it in. This was his medicine to become better and not bitter. The support group is not a psychiatric setting and we were not trying to be or expected to be "fixed," we were being supported, validated and being moved a little forward every time we came. Rhonda & I continued to attend almost every other week. We worked on our statements and began to frame them and they started to take shape and were added to as thoughts would arise. Dr. Bruce guided us in preparing a statement that would be able to be read in court and expressed our impact effectively. I had earlier put together a scrapbook of Marie, and the District Attorney was able to use the pictures during my statement. I was deeply satisfied that I was able to speak on behalf of my sister, myself and our family. I was able to represent her to the jury. It was very healing for me to be able to do that and tell the Jury who she really was and how we loved her very much. In doing so, I also realized that because of the tremendous grief my parents had, they could have never been able to take the stand and read a statement and hold their emotion in, as required. I could see that not all people could fulfill their right to speak on behalf of their loved due to the emotional restraints in place while on the stand.

I was able to work with CVAC and the Douglas County District Attorney's office and many other victims in changing the way victim impact statements are given. I went to the state Capitol of Georgia numerous times to speak to legislators in committees on victim impact testimony. I participated in a judicial study committee and spoke to news media regarding the need to change the way victim impact statements are given. It was an overwhelming success in the House & Senate, not one legislator on either side voted against it. During the week of Victims Rights Week in April 2009 Governor Perdue signed into law giving victims the right to give their statement by prerecorded video, audiotape, or still by reading it. This law also allows more family members to be able to give statements and allows pictures. It was a true victory for the rights of victims and their families. Dr. Bruce, the support group and CVAC helped me accomplish this on behalf of victims. I am now an active board member of CVAC continuing to serve and help other victims of homicide.

As I sat at the grave side service of my sister's funeral, I laid my hand on her coffin and I promised her that I would do everything in my power, will and might to bring her murderer to justice and to always represent her. As long as I have breath, I will continue to do just that.

Norma Jean Hassell

In Memoriam

"What Satan has meant for evil I will turn for good." My name is Norma Jean Hassell. I will begin my story with the event that changed my life and thinking forever. I will not go into how I arrived at this point other than to say that I had strayed far from the path I believe the Lord had laid out for me. I am grateful that He does not throw His blueprints away and that He loved me enough to save me and lead me where I am today.

On December 4, 1987, I was beaten by my live-in boyfriend who I loved with all my heart. I was hospitalized for five days with a concussion, punctured ear drums, and over half of my hair was pulled out. I had a broken rib and punctured lung. I was bruised and swollen from my toes to my fingers to the top of my head. I looked like a monster. I was 5'2" and Mike was 6'3" and 240 pounds. The officer at Northside Hospital said that the person who did this to me must have been a monster. I came home on December 9; Mike had left my home. I could not get him off my mind. I went to church and prayed that God would restore us. I remember praying on the night of my beating while I was still at home, "Lord, You said to praise You in all things." I do not know what to praise You for right now other than I am alive, so I praise You. Mike found another girl friend, but I could not stop praying and seeking a relationship. By the end of 1988 Mike had been incarcerated for beating Gigi.

I saw Mike in September of 1988 and told him that his only hope was in the Lord. On January 15, 1989, I received a phone call from a client. She asked if I had seen the newspaper…there was a small article that said Gigi was dead from blunt trauma to the head. I felt a sick shock to my soul. I went to church and told a friend that, "He has killed Gigi." I prayed all the more and felt led to the verse that says that this kind comes out through prayer and fasting. This seemed counterproductive to me as a recovering anorexic.

By December 1989 I was led to Isaiah 58. My Bible's heading read, "God's acceptable fast!!!" Verse 6 asked if this was not the "fast I have chosen to loose the bands of wickedness, to undo the heavy burdens and let the oppressed go free." I read and studied and meditated on this. I was excited by the implications, but could not see how this could manifest in my world.

Along about March 1990 I was miserable. I could find nowhere to get help with my new feelings, realities, and fears. One day I read an article in the *Gwinnett Daily News* about a free support group for victims of crime operated by CVAC. I went to their next meeting. I began to hear that my fears were "normal" and the sleeplessness and sadness were normal. I was relieved. I still felt that I had "brought this on myself." I did not want to "kill the bum," but" heal the bum." I remember a CVAC therapist telling me that Mike had no reality, but created his own as he went along. What a frightening blow this was to my ego and all my beliefs. How could someone not want a real life? How could I be so vulnerable or naive? I lost confidence in my own judgment.

In March 1991 Mike came out of prison after almost two years and three months for beating a woman, mother, daughter, and fellow human being to death. He was arrested for murder, but plea bargained to second degree involuntary manslaughter by reason of insanity. He spent his time in a medium security state facility, not a mental facility, Mike came to my business and I felt a turning point . . . was he healed, and what do I do?" I wanted him to go away. I called Brooks Hunnicutt, who was running the support group for CVAC, and she advised me to call the DA and Probation officer supervising Mike. That evening I went to church for a revival service. Our visiting minister, who knew nothing of my life, came to me and said, "I believe God would and can rescue you as He would far prefer to bless you." I took this to mean the choice was mine to make. I did not need rescuing again, so I placed Mike in God's hands and walked away.

That same week I received a letter from CVAC asking for volunteer facilitators to assist with running support groups. After training I facilitated support groups for fourteen months in Cobb County with my friend, Diane, for homicide survivors. I also helped to facilitate support groups in Gwinnett County for crime victims. I was trained to answer crisis calls on CVAC's crisis call phone line and did that for two years. Through all this I found a place of service. God knows how to guide us. Through CVAC I learned that crime is not specific to those who "deserve" it. I did not deserve my beating.

I met a man that gave me information that batterers need to change and to recover. Men Stopping Violence (MSV) is an organization for this end. I attended a meeting with Silas Moore, the head of Victim Services for the state Parole Board of Georgia, and Dick Bathrick, the leader of MSV. We discussed what could be done to render aide to domestic violence victims and perpetrators. Soon after this meeting I was privileged to speak to a Senate Judiciary Committee in support of legislation for mandatory education for state incarcerated domestic violence batterers and offenders. This has now become law in Georgia and I believe the Lord through Isaiah 58 enabled me to have a glimpse of this Christian solution to domestic violence.

I believe that battering is a form of addiction. There used to be no help for this addict available, but now a convicted batterer receives nine months of education to point him in a new direction of recovery and restoration. My dream is that if they go back to prison for domestic violence again that there should be a minimum of two years with daily victim impact panels educating and confronting them about their hurtful choices and consequences. When an inmate batterer is released he should learn where he can go to get support for his addiction so he can make a full recovery. If he chooses to batter another victim again he should be placed in a facility for life and perform agricultural or industrial work to avoid being a drain on the state budget. In my dream I would call this program, "Chance for Choice."

I was blessed to receive training, funded by CVAC, with Dr. Joel Brende, a Christian Psychiatrist, whose specialty is Post Traumatic Stress Disorder. He was a part of the Veterans Administration's hospital for 17 years and helped many Vietnam veterans with the disorder. He published several books and has been featured on TV. I learned so much from him about how to understand a trauma victim. I learned how a life can be permanently altered by trauma.

The Bible says "my people perish from the lack of knowledge." Having information which helps me understand my own trauma enables me to see my own and other's dilemma more clearly. This information is power to me and diffuses a lot of the potential harm from trauma. Through CVAC I have seen laws passed over the years and put into place to alter how domestic violence is handled in the system of justice. CVAC was instrumental through Christ to impact the way victims in Georgia and perhaps our country and eventually the whole Earth are seen and cared for through the state and national "Victim's Bill of Rights." I was told the wheels of justice turn slowly but they do turn.

I still have not had a successful male relationship and struggle yet with fear of people. So long as I keep the Lord close in my mind, I do well and improve by overcoming low self-esteem.

The Lord said, "I will cause you to sit among Kings and princes." He has done just that. I praise Him for what He has brought me from and out of and the meaningful organization, CVAC, towards which He has led me.

(Mike died in October 2001. My hope is that he knew the Lord and loved Him and knew of His love for him).

In memoriam: Norma Jean Hassell died of pneumonia in December 2003 from unhealed lung tissue that related to her violent assault of 12/87.

Judge Rowland W. Barnes

My name is Claudia Barnes, and I am now a widow after the senseless and unnecessary murder of my husband, Judge Rowland W. Barnes, at the Fulton County Superior Court in Atlanta, Georgia on March 11, 2005.

When I met Rowland in 1988, I was married with 4 children who ranged in age from 3 to 21. Their dad was 11 years older than me, an alcoholic and a man who was mentally and physically abusive to all of us. I was working at the Fulton County Courthouse in the office of a Magistrate judge, and Rowland was assigned to assist in this position when needed. He was like a breath of fresh air in my life for those few hours, as we became friends who shared the wonderful (and for me, the much needed) gift of laughter. It was also in this job position that I learned about the court system and the types of cases and crimes that came through the doors into the courtrooms. I also learned about confidence in myself and in public speaking.

As an attorney who handled many divorce cases, after about four (4) years I finally asked how a person in my position could ever hope to safely exit a relationship. He put me in touch with a wonderful female lawyer who was there for me every step of the way. Neither Rowland nor myself at that time thought we would ever become more than friends, but we later dated for three (3) years and married. Our first date was on a Friday night at a Mexican restaurant with friends, a date that became a tradition EVERY Friday night. Always exciting and full of fun and laughter, we would begin early in the week asking, "Is it Friday yet?" Our dating was still important to us.

March 11, 2005 was the worst day and worst Friday of my life. Rowland was dreading work that morning, stating he "just wanted to stay in bed and cuddle." It was pretty customary for us to ride to work together, more togetherness time we cherished. But he had to go to work ahead of me this day to go over the jury charges in a rape case - one that was heard a couple or so weeks earlier that ended in a mistrial. After telling me a little bit about the demeanor of the defendant, he said, "I'll see you in a little while, my love. I love you very much." The next time I saw him was at the funeral home when I asked that I be allowed to see his hands and touch them one more time before his body was cremated.

Those words were a constant in my life, along with voice mail messages and spontaneous calls of affection. I loved his voice. So much that after he was murdered, I would play over and over anything I had recorded with his voice attached, all the while crying and outraged that his murder was just not fair. It was also hard to hear special songs on the radio that came at odd times and when least expected.

After another week long trial, the defendant figured out he was going to be found guilty after not being able to manipulate the current jurors. So he decided it was time for him to escape. While being taken to the holding cell to change clothes for court, he pulled the element of surprise over the deputy assigned to escort him, severely beating her to the point that she no longer has the ability to hold a job or live alone — AND, she had two young sons. He took her gun and quickly made his way to my husband's courtroom, quietly slipping into his chambers area, taking hostage two (2) office workers and an attorney and laying wait for the deputy to return.

This evil-hearted defendant with no conscience, one I refer to as Judas, came into the courtroom behind the love of my life, my soulmate, stepped up on his bench a couple of minutes before 9:00 a.m., placed the gun within less than an inch of his head, and shot him. He then turned the gun on his court reporter, shooting her in the same area of her head - a perfect marksman. He looked at the attorney at the Plaintiff's table, who took off running out of the courtroom with the defendant close behind, then ran out and down the stairwell to the outside of the building, crossing a busy street, then turning to shoot and kill that deputy. Many more crimes were committed before he finally shot and murdered a Federal agent who was working on his new home. He received four (4) life sentences, plus 485 years during a trial that lasted three (3) months. I attended all but three (3) days when I attended the marriage of my son and when the military came to move his furniture to his military home. A lot of the evidence presented was almost unbearable to see and hear, but I was there to represent Rowland.

It took almost an hour for me to know that Rowland was for sure the judge who was murdered, and many more hours before I could leave the building to go home. I arrived to total chaos in the street, which was full of persistent and inconsiderate reporters. Thank goodness for my wonderful local police chief, great neighbors and friends. My youngest son, now 19 years of age, was at home alone, and I was very worried about what was going to happen when my 81 year old parents heard the news.

While being shuffled around from place to place in the courthouse, at one point I was handed cards from mental health experts who probably meant well, but to me that was not the time to "talk". It was about a month later that I attended CVAC's candlelight service for victims that Dr. Cook began 20 years ago. I had never been the victim of a murder nor had I ever been a member of a club of this nature that I did not want to join. AND, this was such an emotional service to me. I looked in the faces of all who attended and realized they were still struggling with the loss of loved ones many years later. This made me very nauseated and weak. But when the service ended, I had a peace of heart and mind that only God could have placed there.

GOD MAKES NO MISTAKES. I trust him as my Heavenly Father, and I might never know in this life why this human tragedy was allowed to happen, but if through the death of four (4) dedicated, loving, family-oriented, lovers of freedom and humanity other souls are saved by changes in courthouse procedure and safety or victims are delivered from the heartache and turn to God for healing, then I know without any uncertainty that my husband, Judge Rowland W. Barnes, would have been the first volunteer to help carry out God's plan.

I, personally, have a deep hole in my heart as I now am faced with retirement without the love of my life. We constantly held hands and were together enjoying life that we thought would never end in this manner. What two people and their salaries accomplished together as a perfect team has become a major burden for one. It was not like he had been sick and expected to pass away. After attending the CVAC support group, I realized that I was being called to help other victims through their grieving process, which in turn helps me personally. I am now a member of the Board at CVAC and have chosen to be active in victims' rights by speaking to our Legislative body at the Georgia Capitol about important changes in laws for victims, and I'm proud to say that I have had a great sense of accomplishment by the changes taken place. Too, I've spoken out against domestic violence.

Rowland has been all around me during these trying times. My yard is full of butterflies, mostly orange (his favorite color), cardinals, bluebirds and hummingbirds. Lights flicker and also come and go during gatherings with my friends and family. Practical jokes are played by him, and he sends me many coins along my path, a hobby we enjoyed together. Even an "engagement" ring was outside of my car door on the ground on Valentine's Day. I still buy the weekly flowers that have "that special smell" and were for "my bride."

I want to thank Dr. Cook for his work with, and for, victims of crime, for being there for me and hundreds of others, and for his dedication to healing and setting an example for others that life can go on when we support each other. CVAC is the perfect place for gatherings of the brokenhearted because it is spiritually based. This is the place and the time to realize that our decisions decide our future.

PICTURE NOT AVAILABLE

My name is Angela Sears. My 65 year old Aunt Fannie Mae Tubner and my 74 year old Uncle Johnny Tubner were brutally tortured and murdered in my Ellenwood home on January 23, 2000 by a 15 year old female cousin and three adult male accomplices. It was three thousand seven hundred and one days ago and I have been through one mistrial, two separate jury trials, a death penalty hearing, several appeals in which our family attended. In each court matter we were given bit and pieces of this hellacious and horrific crime.

Reportedly on January 23, 2000 my aunt and uncle had just finished dinner. My aunt was enjoying mini bites of chocolate as she watched television in front of the fireplace. My 15 year old cousin Deandrea Carter knocked on her grandparents; door. She was accompanied by Gregory Fahie and Richard Sealey, while Wajuke Batiste waited in the vehicle parked outside the home. Uncle Johnny opened the door and allowed his granddaughter and the two males access to our home. The large rotwieler which also lived in the home, made his presence known. The guests were unnerved by the dog and appeared to be hesitant to enter the home. Uncle Johnny placed the rotweiler and another dog in the basement and beckoned for the guests to enter. Within minutes the cozy atmosphere warmed by the fireplace would become disdainful and engulfed with violence and death.

Gregory Fahie reports that he requested to use the restroom. Uncle Johnny showed him the way to the restroom and returned to the living room. Gregory Fahie reports hearing a thunderous noise and commotion. Gregory Fahie reports my cousin Deandrea Carter ran up the stairs and exclaimed, "Help me, Dread (Richard Sealey) is fighting with my grandfather" Gregory Fahie reports he attempted to pull Richard Sealey away from my elderly uncle. Richard Sealey managed to pry the gun way from my uncle. My Uncle Johnny was struck in the forehead with his personal handgun. The blunt force trauma to the head knocked my uncle Johnny unconscious, and helpless. Uncle Johnny lay in a pool, of blood which began to seep from the initial head wound. Simultaneously Fannie Mae was also being attacked by Deandrea Carter.

Fannie Mae was enjoying the comforts of home, the warmth of the fireplace and was abruptly startled by the assault on Uncle Johnny. Uncle Johnny shouted for Fannie Mae to shoot as he tussled with Richard Sealey for possession of his weapon. Fannie Mae was unable to take a clear shot with her personal firearm for fear she may have struck Uncle Johnny. Fannie Mae stood in the kitchen with firearm in hand watching her husband being attacked and she too became victimized. Deandrea Carter attacked Fannie Mae, her grandmother, with the fireplace poker. Fannie Mae's arms were secured with electrical duct tape. Fannie Mae was continuously and senselessly tortured. Fannie Mae was kidnapped and dragged through the home in search of money and valuables. Fannie Mae was burned several times with the fireplace poker. She was burned with cigarettes, and her hair was pulled out. She was beaten and kicked on and about her torso and in her face. Fannie Mae repeatedly begged Deandrea Carter and Richard Sealey not to kill her or Uncle Johnny. Horrendous measures were taken to torture Fannie Mae.

Deandrea Carter removed a bandana from her head and placed it in Fannie Mae's mouth and then secured her lips with duct tape. Fannie Mae's eyes were also covered with duct tape the cowardly murderers did not want her to see them end her life. Fannie Mae's feet were also secured with duct tape. Fannie Mae lay on the bed horrified, fearful and overwrought with pain as she encountered five skull shattering blows to her head. Richard Sealey loomed over Fannie Mae in my bedroom as he brought the ax over his head once, twice three times, four times and five times to fatally wound and kill Fannie Mae. What does a granddaughter feel or think as she kills her own flesh and blood, her grandmother? How do you live with yourself? How do you sleep at night?

Gregory Fahie and Deandrea Carter report they both desired to leave and to escape the nightmarish scene of violence and death. Gregory Fahie and Deandrea Carter reported that Richard Sealey told them he would kill them if they did not participate or tried to leave the home before the heinous acts were completed. Unfortunately, the carnage does not end with Fannie Mae. My Uncle Johnny had regained consciousness. Despite blunt force trauma to the head Uncle Johnny attempted to crawl through his own blood. His movement was restricted due to the electrical duct tape placed about his wrists and feet. Before leaving him in a pool of blood Richard Sealey hog tied my Uncle Johnny with duct tape.

The participants reentered the living and dining area to find Uncle Johnny crawling. I believe he was crawling towards help, crawling towards Fannie Mae attempting to save himself, his wife, his family, Deandrea Carter and his legacy. Richard Sealey continued to brutalize my Uncle Johnny as he lay hogtied, bleeding and defenseless. Richard Sealey wielded that ax fifteen times across my Uncle Johnny's skull before he caused irreversible brain damage, a collapsed skull and inevitably death. Each time Richard Sealey wielded that ax to strike another blow he caused the Tubner family anguish, devastation and utter chaos.

The Ellenwood home was ransacked for money and valuables as a husband and wife lay near death and dead. The participants gathered up all of the items they planned to steal and exited the Ellenwood home. The eye from the stove was left on as the smell of burnt skin remained in the air. The television continued to play with no-one to watch. A dying man lay in front of the television moaning. Gregory Fahie reports turning around and hearing my Uncle Johnny moan as he left the Ellenwood home. I can't imagine what my uncle felt or what were his last thoughts?

The participants descended the stairs all with various motives. I am sure they believed by leaving the gas stove on it would erupt in flames and the heinous crime would be obscured by the flames of the fire. Wajuke Batiste reports everyone returned to the car and he sensed something was awry. Reportedly, Gregory Fahie entered the passenger side and reeked of a foul odor. Wajuke Batiste reports he turned around and observed Richard Sealey's and Deandrea Carter's clothes were soaked with blood. Batiste said the stench was unbearable and he became nervous. He reports he attempted to drive off and Richard Sealey informed him Deandrea Carter was hanging out of the car. Deandrea Carter was vomiting. Was she attempting to purge herself of the murders of her sins? Did she feel any remorse? Grim reality stared in the face of a fifteen year old double murderer.

Fannie Mae Tubner and Johnny Tubner were no longer alive; their lifeless bodies lay in a home waiting to be discovered. The Ellenwood home which used to be full of love, warmth and laughter was now vacant and eerily still. The Tubner family lived life as any other night, watched television, ate diner, completed daily living skills and prepared for bed. No one in the Tubner family realized January 24, 2000 would forever change our lives our destiny or our purpose. No one knew except Deandrea Carter.

I was not home at the time of the double homicide. I was in Boston caring for my dying father. January 23, 2000 I returned to my father's condo exhausted from the days events and attempted to call Uncle Johnny and Fannie Mae. I figured they would be watching television. Fannie Mae would be watching a sitcom and Uncle Johnny would be downstairs watching the news. I figured I would speak with Uncle Johnny and Fannie Mae the next day. I wished I had called. I regret not calling them that night. I realize by the compilation of evidence, testimonies and autopsy report they were already dead by 10:00p.m. If I had called there would not have been a happy, loving Tubner on the other end of the phone to accept my long distance call.

The next time I saw Uncle Johnny and Fannie Mae was lying in their caskets during the double funeral. My cousin Eddie Williams and Sheila Williams decided to travel to the Ellenwood home to check on his mother, Fannie Mae and Johnny Tubner. Sheila Williams utilized the family keys and entered the home to find My Uncle Johnny dead, hog tied in a fetal position on the floor. Sheila Williams screamed out and exclaimed, "Someone has killed John." Eddie Williams immediately rushed everyone out of the home. He ran back towards his parents' bedroom in the hope of finding Fannie Mae alive and asleep. Eddie Williams was unable to locate Fannie Mae so he looked in my bedroom. He encountered a gruesome sight. Fannie Mae lay with her skull bashed in, covered in clotted blood and brutalized.

The authorities responded to the call, investigators arrived, police tape covered every inch of the property and the coroners were there, as well. The Tubner and Williams families embraced, cried and stood in anguish and amazement for nine hours as they waited for answers, for someone to make sense of this horrific act for someone to pinch them and to say wake up. I felt I was dreaming.

I open my eyes to a cold still house and I realize a piece of my heart and my home is empty. The warm, comfortable and safe environment I used to enjoy has been destroyed by deviant acts of violence. I actually can't even call my three bedroom apartment a home. I was forced to leave my sanctuary my safety net several years ago. The perpetration of a horrific double homicide caused my world to become grief filled and chaotic.

I want to introduce you to Johnny Tubner and Fannie Mae Tubner as I knew them, the aunt and uncle I loved and will always remember. My Uncle Johnny was a simple, humble loving spirit. He was a deacon of his church, a great father, loving grandfather, brother, uncle, stepfather, husband and friend. Uncle Johnny enjoyed being the patriarch of the family, working, volunteering and spending quality time with his family. I would often chastise my uncle for speaking to strangers and being too friendly. My uncle always managed to see the world through rose colored glasses, always striving to see the good in everyone and somehow managing to ignore the character flaws and defects.

I don't ever recall a moment wherein my uncle was not smiling, humming, laughing or making someone else laugh. I think of his memory and all I can do is smile through the dissipating pain, my reality that I will never feel his touch again. My uncle Johnny enjoyed life and managed to touch each individual's path he crossed. Uncle Johnny was too friendly and giving that actually evoked me to voice my concerns about his willingness to give. He always wore several gold necklaces, 8 diamond rings and a beautiful diamond watch on his wrist. I often felt like strangers would take his kindness for weakness. My Uncle Johnny addressed my concerns and he assured me we would be safe, we would be safe. He said, "Baby we will be alright. I have this gun on my hip. I am not worried about folks bothering us. We are good people and they can only be good to us. I want you to remember something…..if I pull this gun out of the holster I plan to use it. I am going to shoot and I will shoot to kill if I have to protect myself, you or my family."

I forced myself to disregard the nagging sense of trepidation and fear I felt. I loved my Uncle Johnny. In my eyes he could do no wrong and he was always right. I wanted to believe that things would be alright but I didn't have on those rose colored glasses he wore. In that moment I was his baby. We embraced each other exchanged "I love yous" and enjoyed each other's company.

Aunt Fannie Mae was quite the character. Stereotypically a large number of women lie about their age and their weight. I am not quite sure of either number for Fannie Mae's age or weight and she would often prod me and joke about my obesity. Fannie Mae was a loving mother, wife, grandmother, sister, aunt and friend. Fannie Mae was determined, hardworking, purpose driven and dependable. I would often accompany Fannie Mae to various work sites. I enjoyed getting to know her and I became to love her as my Uncle Johnny loved her. Fannie Mae and I would often talk about the future and their plans for retirement and beneficiary terms. I would be hesitant to listen and often times I would half heartedly listen and rush to change the subject. I didn't want to discuss a time where I would have to live without my Uncle Johnny or my aunt Fannie Mae. We marveled in the thoughts of my Uncle Johnny being able to love us both so strongly. Fannie Mae embraced me and told me she loved me.

    I will fast forward to 5p.m.on January 24, 2000, my world, my reality. I received a call at the nurses' station from my aunt Liz. Liz asked me to come to her home once I left my father at the rehabilitation facility. I had an awful feeling in the pit of my stomach and my extremities went numb. My mind began to race and I thought of all the family members in Atlanta, Alabama, Florida and all over. I wondered who had died, who was hurt or who had been killed in a car accident or had a heart attack. Death had knocked on our door previously that year. I had lost my cousin on Wednesday, my aunt on Thursday and my mom on Saturday. I had prepared myself for another death. I knew on 10/03/1998 something horrific was to come. I never imagined a double homicide would validate my innermost fears. I couldn't concentrate or really care take of my father. I excused myself and left early. I prayed all the way to my Aunt Liz's home. I asked God for strength, courage and understanding. I approached my Liz's home and she was waiting for me at the top of the stair case. I thought how odd? I remember telling her to allow me to use the restroom and to unwind. I opened the door to find her centered in the doorway of the bathroom. I asked her what was wrong." Immediately my throat began to tighten, my heart began to palpitate and my mind was racing. Liz said, "I am not going to b.s you. I have bad news. Someone broke in the house last night and killed Uncle Johnnie and Fannie Mae.

The sound which escaped me cannot be described by words. An indistinct bellow of anguish and despair flowed from my lips. I can remember my aunt's face and I remember her lips moving but I can't remember the words she uttered. I sat down to gather myself and to ask questions. The phone began to ring as everyone questioned Liz about my response to the news. I asked my Aunt Rosia who resides in Atlanta and who had actually observed the crime scene, "What happened?" Hysterically Rosia attempted to answer but she just blurted out, "There was so much blood."

Speculation began and the investigation ensued. The Tubner family members blamed the Williams family members and vice versa. The local authorities reported there weren't any signs of forced entry and reported the murderer or murderers were allowed access to the Ellenwood home. I won't spend much time on painting a picture of the double funeral. Imagine death times two. Attempt to make sense of a senseless act.

I can't begin to rationalize the past events. Oddly enough, I feel anxious and unnerved when someone speaks about Super bowl events. I have negative associations related to the particular weekend. Everyone in Atlanta traveled around town to various homes, sites and parties anticipating the fulfilled activities of traditional pregame, and post game events. I was overwhelmed with the mere notion of attending a double funeral. The reality of the senseless and horrific deaths would soon enough haunt me. Words cannot describe the pain, agony, anger, frustration and emptiness embodied in my spirit, my physical body within my soul as I walked away from the burial site Super bowl weekend.

I was faced with harsh reality, my family was gone. I would no longer be Uncle Johnny's baby. I would no longer hear Fannie Mae laugh. I would no longer be able to laugh with them. We wouldn't be able to share loving fulfilled moments. Once Uncle Johnny and Fannie Mae were laid to rest the drama ensued. One can only imagine the crisis to unfold.

Deandrea Carter was the initial person to be connected to the case. Deandrea Carter was held by local authorities due to her unruly behavior/run away status. During the initial apprehension of Deandrea Carter the local authorities also placed Richard Sealey under arrest. The local authorities were led to a pay by the week hotel where Deandrea Carter resided with her boyfriend Richard Sealey. The local authorities obtained a search warrant for the hotel room and secured evidence. The evidence collected led to a third participant named Wajuke Batiste. Wajuke Batiste was apprehended, questioned and detained for his participation in the double homicide. Lastly, Gregory Fahie was detained in the Virgin Islands and transported back to Atlanta for his participation in the double homicide. Four defendants were questioned, interrogated, detained, charged and arraigned for a jury trial. Our family participated in several bond hearings and court proceedings before attending a jury trial.

I can share with you my experience in secondary victimization and the lack of awareness amongst law enforcement agents. I recall a bond hearing wherein Wajuke Batiste and Gregory Fahie had family members attend the proceedings. The courtroom in Lovejoy was not large enough to accommodate the number of people in attendance. The presiding judge looked up and into the group of Nubian faces and said, "There are too many of them in here. They have to leave." I can remember being shocked and infuriated. I could not believe a judicial person had acted in such a callous manner. I wasn't sure to be angry in regards to the number of people which appeared to support a murderer or to be angry with the judge for being so rude. Nevertheless, I was severely impacted. My thoughts of the judicial system were tainted. I began to question the legal system. I wondered if our family would receive justice. I wondered if their deaths would be in vain. I wondered if people would see Johnnie Tubner and Fannie Mae Tubner as precious gifts, precious loved ones or would they be remembered as the elderly African American couple murdered in Ellenwood. I struggled with the notion my family would be discriminated against because the legal system would not take the time to see Uncle Johnny and Fannie Mae as I knew them. I prayed to the Lord that this cannot be happening. We are in the twentieth century. We are in the year 2000. I looked around the grounds of the Lovejoy facility while praying as the Confederate flag flew.

Eventually the justice system did act. They were found guilty. I wish I could say it is all over but now over ten years later I am still a work in progress. I am the secretary for the Board of Directors of

CVAC and I have spoken out for crime victims on TV. I attended support groups to work on my feelings after the double murder. I help plan for and conduct a memorial service for crime victims every April. I have pushed for legislative changes to help crime victims. I will heal with God's help.

These stories from crime survivors show that people who survive a murder or vehicular homicide are in incredibly deep pain, anger and depression. They grieve intensely from the incident of murder and the secondary forms of victimization that arise from the criminal justice process. The faith community can be there to support them through this grieving process in prayer, individual and group sessions led by clergy and trained volunteers that facilitate their journey towards recovery.

Chapter 9

THE ROLE OF CHAPLAIN

As a chaplain I found myself in the role of extension ministries within the connectional structure of the United Methodist Church. My Bishop appointed me every year to serve in a jail, prison or crime victim's chaplaincy and I was endorsed by the United Methodist Endorsing Agency. I never felt alone, because of all the support I received at Annual Conferences and by UMEA staff who were truly wonderful, caring people. At times I must admit I knew I was in the body of Christ, but I felt like a hangnail I was so far out. It is a long way from being a pastor in a church to counseling an inmate in D block after his mother died and he cannot go home or listening to the rage of a mother whose only son was killed at the precise moment she was praying at the sink for his protection. I also had seventeen years in which I ran two halfway houses for the Georgia Department of Corrections, worked as a corrections specialist for the LEAA regional office in Atlanta or worked as a parole examiner for the U.S. parole Commission which shaped many of my views about criminals. Being a chaplain was the bookends of my career and the other jobs were sandwiched in between. I think those other jobs made me a unique chaplain.

Drew Theological School prepared me to be a minister and I took memorable courses that helped me shape my theology: Dave Graybeal's Search for the Good Community; Tom Oden's class on sensitivity training; Nelle Morton's Christian Education classes;

Nelson Thayer's class on pastoral care; Lynne Westfield's class about Oppression; Leonard Sweet's class on technology and theology. Michael Christensen and Carl Savage were inspirational. My dissertation for my doctorate at Drew was called *Justice That Reconciles and Heals*. It is available for free from www.cvaconline.org. I also studied in New York City in Human Relations and took Transactional Analysis courses under Dr. Mary Boulton, who studied with Eric Berne. I took a family systems course from Peggy Papp of the Nathan Ackerman Family Institute. I studied psychodrama with Hannah Weiner of the Moreno Institute for Psychodrama and the Virginia Satir model of family therapy from Ruth Ann Pippenger. I was supervised in Atlanta by Dr. James Kilgore for AAMFT supervision. Elaine Gibson was my AAMFT personal counselor. Some chaplains become licensed professional counselors, or LPCs, and some become licensed social workers, or LCSWs. An endorsed prison or crime victim's chaplain also needs to determine if one or two years of clinical pastoral education (CPE) is required to fill the job.

Dr. "Mickey" Burglass was a profound influence on shaping the way I viewed criminal behavior as a choice the criminal makes. Bluewolf taught me the Talking Stick, which is the most therapeutic technique for healing I have ever used. Harmon Wray taught me restorative justice programs, and I enjoyed serving with him on the UMC Restorative Justice Task Force for four years. We held five seminars around the country, and I did seminars on crime victims and restorative justice ministry with Harmon. I wrote a piece for Harmon in his restorative justice manual which was published.

OVC trained me in Victims Assistance Training online, in a *Train the Trainer* course and in a *Mental Health Response to Mass Violence and Terrorism* course. ICISF trained me in a course involving pastoral care intervention for crime victims. I was a member of NOVA and presented a NOVA seminar in Atlanta on how to run a homicide co-victims support group. I joined the American Correctional Association's Protestant Chaplain's association and served on the ACA Task Force on Victims of Crime for four years which issued national recommendations for corrections to improve services for crime victims. I was a reviewer of the Faith-based Recommendations in the 1998 *New Directions from the Field* published by OVC. Because of all this education and training I was enabled to facilitate prisoners and crime victims to help themselves and to promote their healing but not on my own. God was guiding me and strengthening me all the time.

The most important element of healing was though prayer. Without prayer I would have been a tinkling cymbal. Over time and week to week the prayers to God were the glue that makes the healing stick. I thank God for the way He answers the prayers. I saw miraculous turnarounds through the weekly prayer in a homicide co-victim's support group. I did 500 homicide co-victim's support groups (about 50 a year for ten years) on Tuesday evenings at the Vinings UMC. Most of the time there were only 4 or 5 of us, but the transformation from a grieving, enraged or severely depressed homicide co-victim to a person who felt confident such that they could cope with the loss and assimilate the murder into their own life in such a way that they could now deal with it—that is an amazing miracle to watch. They had to change in such a way that they could reconstruct their entire life with a sense of transformed meaning after their loved one was killed. They would never be "normal" again after the murder, but would be a new form of normal. They would not have what some call "closure," but they would have an adjusted sense of healing over time. Sometimes they got better and sometimes they got worse, but they did get through both ups and downs with some coping skills that we taught in the group. I was privileged to witness remarkable resilience.

When crime victims have a "trigger" that causes them to flash back and relive the moment of the crime, they can go into a panic or anxiety mode and have trouble breathing. It is called a panic attack, and we taught a breathing exercise in the group that slowed the heartbeat so the panic attack would diminish. The reason we taught this relaxation and breathing exercise is based on the very low scores on the Coping Skills tests, usually in the 50s range, on the category of "ability to relax." The opening prayer of the support group calmed them. Then the relaxation exercise further calmed them. Then the talking stick go-around enabled all to talk until finished, and this calmed them to be able to "talk out" all the pain and hurt and anger.

The homicide co-victim's personal narrative, or story, was brutal since it involved murder, and they needed to tell that story to someone in the support group who could not only listen but partially understand since a similar murder happened to them as well. Then the group dealt with issues they were facing: how to write a victim impact statement: fill out a victims comp form: write the parole board: get a civil suit started: handle problems at work, with family or friends who said things about the murder that upset the group member. Then the group ended with a circle prayer.

Rudolf Bultmann calls it "sitz im leben" which means situation in life. A chaplain faces a situation in life when he has a prisoner, a soldier or soldier's family member, a hospital patient, a police officer, a pastoral care client, a victim of violent crime, a hospice patient, a life coach or workplace client, and they are looking to the chaplain as a man of God to help them cope. These hearts, minds and souls are looking for and sometimes crying out for help from a person in the role of a chaplain. It is also within the context of the environmental situation in life that you are facing at the time as a chaplain that tests your faith and skill to be a caring presence for that person who needs your help. For example, a military chaplain faces issues of young men and women placing themselves in harm's way when they could die in battle or a roadside bomb and the chaplain may be deployed to the same location as the man who needs his help. The chaplain has to deal with his own fears, loneliness and doubts at the time he is expected to help the soldier with his. The chaplain preaches, offers sacraments, counsels with and prays with the soldier for God and country. The chaplain is there for his soldiers and is a spiritual and physical presence that represents faith in God in times of trouble.

A hospital chaplain faces issues of death and dying and serious diseases every day. He hears patient fears of dying and being in terrible pain and must offer prayers, consoling and comforting words, and be a minister of caring presence at the same time that he must be careful to not catch the same communicable disease that the dying patient has. The same is true of a hospice chaplain. He prays and offers Christ and the resurrected Christ to the patients as a source of eternal rest and hope in Christ that the patient may die in this world but will meet Christ in the next. He is the face of the church when he tells a family their son has died. A campus chaplain, workplace chaplain and police chaplain all have their own contexts, too.

The jail or prison or the support group room—these were my contexts. Standing against the wall at mainline during chow in prison so inmates could ask me questions was my context as a prison chaplain. Walking and talking was common. During crime victims crisis calls the telephone was my context. The memorial service and lighting candles for lost loved ones was my context. Touching the shoulder of a weeping widow whose husband was murdered was my context. Fighting for laws that support the rights of crime victims in my state and on the federal level was my context as a crime victims' chaplain.

A chaplain stands in the gap. The church is a long way from Iraq or Afghanistan, the hospital bed of a dying man, D block, or the tearful face of a grieving mother whose only child was murdered at 19 years of age. I felt at times like I was the long arm of the church that reached all the way into that jail, prison or support group room to offer Christ to whoever would accept Him. I do not have the authority to heal, but Christ does. I have skills, but Christ will use them in the best way when I am acting as His agent and His messenger. I ministered to Muslim, Jew and Christian alike and to atheist or agnostic.

I had to learn about limits and boundaries and live within the parameters of the professional ethics of my profession, AAMFT, and professional standards for victim advocates. When I was a federal prison chaplain I was also required to obey the Department of Justice code of conduct. I knew I had limits and by law had to report child abuse, elder abuse, and if the client said he wanted to kill himself or others or destroy government property. I knew as a chaplain I had a higher moral standard based on my role.

Both as a prison and crime victim's chaplain I honored confidentiality and did not violate it. I had to be a pluralist chaplain that respected and supported all faiths or no faith in various clients. I did not proselytize but would respond if invited to witness for my faith. When I ran support groups I always said the prayer before and after the group was voluntary and separated in time, and sometimes space, from the group. No one was forced to attend the prayer time and some came a bit late and left early to avoid it and that was fine. I ended prayer with, "In God's holy name I do pray." For me God's holy name is Jesus Christ, but if I had a Muslim or Jewish person in the support group I wanted them to feel comfortable. Federal funds cannot be used for prayer time, worship, scripture study, or proselytizing. Federal funds cannot be used to require a crime victim to attend a religious event to receive services and discrimination on the basis of religion and other matters is prohibited.

After a murder of an officer in federal prison I experienced vicarious trauma and compassion fatigue and needed help. I got it from an outside counselor, my pastor, my wife, family, friends and faith community. I received more healing than I deserve from the homicide co-victims support group that met every Tuesday night for ten years. I thank God for each of them. Their resilience and coping helped me to cope. The prayers and comments were so healing. The Vinings United Methodist Church helped me and my ministry for crime victims with their prayers, support, free space and constant encouragement.

I learned real ministry from the victims' advocates in the DA offices. They stand in the gap and offer comfort, accurate information and physical presence to crime victims and take the place of missing clergy in our courthouses. My challenge is for clergy or lay leaders of churches, synagogues, tribes, temples and mosques who are reading this to say, where do I sign up? I want to be there to help crime victims, too. Where do I sign up? I want to be a prison volunteer.

Victim service agencies and prisons are not hard to find, just hard to find time to serve. Can you find the time?

CONCLUSION:
A CALL TO ACTION

It is not possible to make America into an Inn of healing for all crime victims overnight, but it is possible to get started on it by taking some practical steps.

The nation's workforce of crime victims' chaplains

The Office for Victims of Crime (OVC) could recruit, train and supervise 50 crime victims chaplains recommended by the Governors of 50 states and deliver a cadre of 2,500 trained and certified crime victims' chaplains. This cadre would be immediately available in the event of a mass terrorism attack and would work during the year with each victim advocate at the local, state and federal levels of the courts and judiciary. The training would occur each year at each location of the National Victim Assistance Academy and would be funded by OVC and the individual states. The Office of Faith-based Services in the White House would serve as coordinator of a national crime victims chaplaincy and the Director of all chaplains would be housed in the Executive Office of the U. S. Attorney in Washington, D.C. Continued training for crime victims chaplains would occur at National Organization of Victims Assistance (NOVA) and National Center for Victims of Crime Conferences. An online version of the training would be developed by OVC TTAC similar to Victim Assistance Training currently offered but it would be modified for crime victim's chaplaincy. A dedicated web site at OVC would be developed for crime victim's chaplains to interface and network.

This would get us started. Each of the trained chaplains would develop a resource list of churches, synagogues, tribes and mosques that would be willing to help crime victims with resources such as finding a job after a wage earner is disabled or killed in a crime, or relocating a victim after stalking or domestic violence abuse. The chaplains would attend court with crime victims they counseled and help to insure their needs for transportation and safety and comfort were met. The chaplains would be on contract or volunteer status to help the city and county District Attorney VWAPs and the U.S. ATTY VWAPs with their crime victims who attend court.

Each major denomination would offer a course on Crime Victims Chaplaincy in at least one of their seminaries or theological schools. Seminaries would offer the Denver Seminary course curriculum on victim care for each denomination and modify and improve it over time with OVC seed money. The seminary could offer a course on chaplaincy or extension ministries but they would be required to teach a large portion of it for crime victims chaplaincy similar to the Denver Seminary model in order to obtain the seed money from OVC.

Crime victims' rights

Each state should have a crime victim's bill of rights that is enforceable if not complied with. All states have a listing of crime victims' rights but they are more like a suggestion than a right if not complied with. If there is no way to enforce the right after it was denied it really was not a right to begin with. I worked on Georgia's crime victim bill of rights in the late 80's and I worked on supporting the federal Crime Victims Rights Act of 2005 which is enforceable by a writ of mandamus if not complied with in the federal courts. I recently worked on House Bill 567 which passed in Georgia which would give us remedies with the Judicial Qualifications Commission if our crime victim right was denied. For example, if you are the surviving family member of a murder in Georgia and your right to a give a victim impact statement at the sentencing phase of the murder trial was either denied or ignored you currently have no remedy for that. If the law were changed and you had a right to go to a higher court of appeals and ask for a "redo" of that then you would ask that the appeals judge order the offender back into the court for you to provide your victim impact statement in front of him and the sentencing judge. Then, a person's right to provide a victim impact statement at sentencing is safeguarded and exercised. This is very important to a crime victim and contributes to their healing when they deliver these victim impact statement. I have counseled some whose crime victim's rights were ignored and it was very hurtful for them to experience that. Personally, I like Arizona's model for remedial action and we used some of that language in Georgia's HB 567. Each crime victim and citizen can change laws to promote the rights of crime victims. It is a citizen's right and duty to promote fairness in our courts. I also worked with many other advocates on passing SB 452 in Georgia which permitted audio-visual forms of victim impact statements at sentencing. We also supported a bill to improve restitution and two bills to approve notification procedures for crime victims in Georgia.

Restorative justice models

Restorative justice models should be attempted in all adult and juvenile non-violent cases in which the victim and offender agreed to the mediation. Prosecutors would agree to try restorative justice mediation for adult and juvenile non-violent offenses which would enable them to spend more time on serious, violent cases. This would require starting small in each court of limited jurisdiction and expanding to the district trial courts as the program staff and utilization grew.

Crime victimization course

Offenders should be required to complete a 120-hour course on crime victimization while incarcerated. Victim-impact statements already available as videos would be viewed by inmates so that they could understand the impact of their crime upon the victims and their families. Materials from Mothers Against Drunk Driving, Parents of Murdered Children, America's Most Wanted missing and exploited children, to name a few, can be developed as instruction for the 120-hour course on victimization. One of the biggest criticisms I have of corrections is that they do not encourage the offender to take responsibility for the impact of his crimes while incarcerated. Consequently, the offender does not think much about the crime and how he hurt crime victims but just wants to get out as soon as possible. By viewing victim impact videos in prison he could increase his sensitivity to the harm he caused which could make him re-offend less.

Inmate financial responsibility

Select offenders who have good conduct and are within 10 years of release would be able to earn minimum wage working for vendors who come into the prison, or in house prison developed industries, and the offenders would pay 25% of their wages to a crime victims fund, or specific crime victim if known, 25% to federal and state taxes, and 25% for room and board and 25% for himself (commissary account) and to send home to his family. My good friend, Dr. J. Price Foster, a criminal justice professor, used to say, "If it is programmatically important it should be administratively possible."

Currently, Prison Industries Employment, or PIE programs, operate in 37 states but the range and cap on victims' funds is 5 to 20% that can go to crime victims from inmate wages in the PIE program. Most participating states have their offenders paying about 8% to crime victims on the average. The sea change here is to see that offenders should be paying their crime victims they hurt first and foremost. Therefore, the figure should be 25% of their inmate wages paid to crime victims.

Say an inmate makes widgets inside the prison walls for Widgets Inc. and he earns $12,000 a year from minimum wages. This would mean that $3000 would go to a victims fund or the specific victim if crime-related losses were established to be $3000. Every time he received his pay and it was garnered to go to the crime victim he would have to think of the one he harmed. That restitution could help the crime victim recover financially from the loss he suffered at the hands of the criminal.

Restitution needs to be improved.

Victim advocates, probation officers, parole officers, crime victims, prosecutors, judges, crime victims' chaplain—no one I have talked to is happy with the inept way restitution is handled in this country. It is at the heart of any real restorative justice and yet it is so poorly accounted for that in Georgia they could not even find a crime victim to pay them restitution when they were located in the building one floor below the Department of Corrections according to Jody Fleischer, investigative reporter of WSB TV. They had hundreds of thousands of dollars, but could not locate the crime victims and, therefore, called it abandoned restitution. By state law DOC was supposed to send the restitution on to the Criminal Justice Coordinating Council victim's fund after two years but had not done so until prompted by Ms Fleischer. Ms. Fleischer located many of the "un-locatable" crime victims by going on the Internet and typing in their name. The GA DOC put in protocols and policies to improve this condition recently.

Every state correctional agency responsible for collecting restitution for crime victims should be monitored and audited for fiscal responsibility every two years. Adequate staff and training of staff needs to be marshaled to collect restitution owed to crime victims. Each crime victim should have an account set up to check off the owed amounts until it is paid. If the restitution was ordered by the court the judge and his clerk should monitor it to see that it was paid as well. If the Parole Board ordered the restitution it should be monitored monthly to insure it was paid.

Offenders should be required to pay restitution and community service in all cases for which documented crime-related losses were proven. If the sentence was probation, a sentence of time, a parole release, a diversion program, a halfway house stay and even while incarcerated the offender should be asked to pay a fair portion of his earnings to the victim for restitution. Failure to make a diligent effort to pay restitution when resources are evident would be grounds for an offender who is in the community to be placed in a halfway house for up to 120 days.

When a crime victim receives restitution and it is de-emphasized and only a nickel to a half dollar on the dollar is paid with little or no consequence to the offender it is patently unfair. In fact, if anyone should go into debt to pay restitution it should be the offender, and not the victim, who owes the debt directly attributable to the crime. Therefore, I concur with the recommendations below made by OVC's *New Directions from the Field*, which states:

> "Across the country, some jurisdictions are using innovative strategies to collect restitution when offenders fail to pay on schedule. These efforts include using civil remedies, making offenders forfeit bond money for restitution obligations, collecting restitution while offenders are institutionalized as well as after they are placed on parole, providing incentives for incarcerated offenders to pay restitution, accepting credit card payments, garnishing wages, converting restitution orders to community service, extending community supervision until offenders fulfill their restitution obligations, and hiring private collection agencies to seek payment. These innovative methods are discussed below in further detail.

Civil Remedies

According to the National Victim Center, 41 states have laws that provide civil remedies for victims whose offenders' sentences include restitution orders. In most of these states, once an offender has defaulted on payment, a civil judgment can be enforced by placing a lien on real property, garnishing wages, attaching assets or wages, or freezing bank accounts. The attachment of deposited funds ("freezing") is usually time-limited from the initial restitution order (such as 24 months), unless it is extended by the court or paroling authority.

Laws in several states provide for specific measures to enforce restitution orders as civil judgments. Delaware allows up to one-third of an offender's total earnings to be assigned to victim restitution. Minnesota and Washington provide for the freezing of bank accounts, and courts in Montana and Oklahoma may order the forfeiture, seizure, or sale of offenders' assets.

Forfeiture of Bond Money

In Westchester County, New York, when a violation of probation is filed as a result of failure to pay restitution, the probation officer can request bail. The officer then suggests that the court set bail in the amount of the owed restitution, if the amount is not unreasonable. In the accompanying report to the court, the court is advised that if the violation is sustained and the probationer is willing to assign the bail money as payment of restitution, the probation department would recommend that probation be continued or, in some cases, terminated.

The report recommends alternative sentences for probationers who will not assign bail money. These sanctions modify the order to include a graduated sanction such as "shock time," community service, or electronic monitoring. In some instances, a recommendation of revocation and a sentence of incarceration are made.

Restitution Collection in Institutions

Many forward-looking correctional agencies encourage inmates' participation in fulfilling their restitution obligations and increase collections by offering incentives. Correctional agencies use a variety of measures to do this, including increasing inmates' privileges for visitation and services at the prison commissary, giving them priority enrollment in popular education programs, and removing privileges for failure or refusal to participate in the department's victim restitution program. Restitution program staff and court officials must be educated on the availability of prison restitution procedures.

The California Department of Corrections (CDC) has implemented an Inmate Restitution Fine Collections System supported by state law that enables the department to deduct up to 50 percent of inmate wages and other trust account deposits to pay court-ordered restitution. This amount is forwarded to the State Board of Control Restitution Fund, which provides reimbursement to qualified victims for expenses such as medical costs and counseling incurred as a result of the crimes committed against them. Since its inception in November 1992, this system has resulted in the collection of over $9 million from inmate wages and trust account deposits. CDC's Victim Services Program staff also coordinates voluntary restitution payments from inmates and parolees as well as money from annual inmate fundraising events.

Community Restitution

When offenders are truly indigent and unable to pay even a portion of their restitution order, many correctional agencies give offenders the option of performing community restitution. It should only be imposed, however, after victims have given their consent. Some victims may want to have the restitution order remain in effect for the offender's lifetime rather than see their debt discharged in another fashion. Other victims may feel a measure of compensation by helping to select the type and location of the service that offenders will perform. Offenders generally perform services directly for the victim, for a favorite charity of the victim, or a public work project of the agency that the victim chooses. Victim restitution does not preclude an order of community restitution as well. The offender not only has caused monetary damage to the victim but also has damaged the safety and security of the community as a whole.

Using Private Collection Agencies

Some states authorize justice agencies to use the services of private collection agencies to secure restitution payments. The use of private collection agencies, which have experience, automated systems, and employees trained to track down delinquent debtors, can significantly increase the collection of restitution. Although a percentage of the payment collected is kept by the collection agency, reducing the amount of restitution the victim receives. Many justice agencies and victims feel that 90 percent of a restitution order is better than nothing at all. When contracting for the services of private collection agencies, justice agencies should establish clear guidelines for acceptable collection tactics and secure the permission of the victim.

Victim Services, Inc., a nonprofit organization, manages the restitution collection program in New York City for all non-probation cases. In fiscal year 1997, 2,732 cases were referred to the organization, which collected a total of $1,830,000. Overall, the payment rate in those cases was 79 percent.

Enforcing Restitution Statutes

Several states and local jurisdictions have undertaken innovative measures to enforce restitution orders. In some states, offenders who fail to pay restitution risk being held in contempt of court, imprisoned, or having their parole or probation extended or revoked. Such sanctions can be lifted in extreme cases in which an offender can demonstrate hardships that prevent them from making payment. However, in such cases, restitution payment schedules should be adjusted, not abandoned. It is important that victims understand their obligation to report non-payment of court-and parole board-ordered restitution so that correctional agencies can assess the reasons for nonpayment and consider sanctions. Victims should be provided the opportunity to have input into the types of sanctions that might be imposed.

Recommendations from the Field for Restitution from OVC's *New Directions from the Field 1998*

Restitution Recommendation from the field #1

Restitution orders should be mandatory and consistent nationwide. Full restitution should include all immediate and expected monetary costs of the crime to victims, including property loss, health and mental health costs, and, when appropriate, compensation for pain and suffering. When a victim cannot be identified to receive restitution, judges should consider ordering payment to national, state, or local victim assistance or compensation programs. Judges should review restitution orders periodically to assess whether the victim has incurred additional costs as a result of the crime and whether the offender is making timely payments. Restitution payment plans should include provisions for immediate payment of full restitution should the offender obtain additional financial assets. Judges should order full restitution in every case. Realistic payment schedules should be established, and victims should be advised fully about realistic expectations for the likelihood and speed of full collection. Restitution orders should reflect the full extent of damages to the victim so that victims can seek civil judgments in that amount.

Restitution Recommendation from the field #2

A coordinated, interagency response throughout the justice system is essential for the effective collection of restitution. It is critical that all justice agencies responsible for restitution, including courts, probation, prosecution, and corrections, implement coordinated, interagency models for the collection of restitution to enable professionals at each stage of the process to carry out their responsibilities more effectively. Much of the disparity between the perceived and actual effectiveness of restitution practices may be traced to procedures that have become cumbersome because they involve numerous agencies and personnel. A coordinated interagency approach to restitution collection that manages this complex process with clearly defined roles and streamlined tasks will improve communication among agencies, increase consultation and communication with victims, and enforce judicial restitution orders with appropriate follow through.

Restitution Recommendation from the field #3

Restitution must be a priority for all criminal justice agencies if it is to be implemented successfully. Because multiple entities are involved throughout the restitution process, successful collection depends on their ability to cooperate. Studies show that compliance increases when restitution is made a priority in correctional agencies, but lags when restitution is not a top agency concern. Programs that aggressively target restitution generate more successful performances and lower recidivism rates.

Restitution Recommendation from the field #4

Victims should be informed as early as possible in the justice process of their right to receive restitution from the offender. They should be notified of the disposition of the case, advised of realistic expectations for payment, and provided with information about their rights when offenders fail to pay.

Because many victims are not informed of their right to obtain restitution for their losses, they do not adequately document their financial losses. Without this evidence, victims have a difficult time proving damages at the time of sentencing. Victims should be informed of their right to restitution as early as possible, and they should receive information at that time on what type of documentation is necessary for the court and what methods they can use to obtain that documentation. In addition, victims should be informed of whom to call if they have any problems or questions. The appropriate agencies must initiate proceedings in those jurisdictions which provide for statutory imposition of civil remedies.

Restitution Recommendation from the field #5

At the time of sentencing, courts should have sufficient information about both the victim and the offender to determine the amount of full restitution and a payment schedule. Judges often state that their failure to order restitution is due to a lack of information regarding the victim's loss or the offender's financial assets or future ability to pay. Presentencing reports must contain victim impact information on financial losses, including current and expected medical and counseling expenses, lost wages, and property losses.

Presentencing reports should also cover offenders' ability to pay restitution, including information on wages accumulated while incarcerated pending trial or final sentencing. Moreover, victim impact statements should describe the cost of the crime to the victim, particularly in cases in which a presentence investigation report was not filed.

Justice professionals and victim service providers also have a responsibility to educate victims about how to document immediate losses such as expenses related to medical care, mental health services, funeral expenses, time off from work, and crime scene cleanup and relocation. The guidelines for documenting losses for restitution orders that were developed through the National Victim Center's Promising Practices and Strategies for Victim Services in Corrections project sponsored by the Office for Victims of Crime should be widely distributed to victims.

Restitution Recommendation from the field #6

The use of technology can greatly enhance the tracking and payment of restitution orders. Those responsible for monitoring restitution should automate their program. The full automation of restitution collection will assure more efficient communication among responsible agencies and improve the tracking of money collected, owed, and disbursed. Many jurisdictions are creating software packages that fully automate restitution processes, which substantially increases both restitution collection and victim satisfaction.

One reason restitution orders are not enforced is the cost involved in tracking the orders. Automation can improve efficiency and, over time, greatly reduce this cost. One software package, for example, includes programs for tracking payments, establishing disbursement priorities, prompting enforcement measures and generating enforcement reports, and writing checks to victims. To facilitate the collection of restitution, administrative fees should be included in any order that includes payment in installments. These fees should be used to develop computerized tracking systems or to prioritize collection.

Restitution Recommendation from the field #7

Offenders should be held accountable for restitution payments; state legislation should make restitution payments a priority over other payments due from the offender, including fines, fees, and restitution to entities other than the crime victim; and restitution payments should be collected before fines or penalties.

Correctional agencies should put procedures in place for dealing with offenders who fail to pay restitution as ordered. When offenders fail to make restitution payments, notice should be sent to the appropriate judicial or probation officers to reevaluate the offenders' ability to pay and their release status. Measures that can be taken in response to offenders who default on payments range from informal communication by the probation officer to a court-ordered revocation hearing. When appropriate, the probation officer should consider steps to modify the payment schedule. If an action is taken that will affect the payment of restitution, the victim should be informed. When an offender's probationary period is coming to a close and an outstanding balance of restitution remains, the probation department or the court should extend supervision, step up collection, or assist victims with procedures to pursue civil judgments.

Offenders are generally unable to pay all restitution, fines, court fees and other costs in one lump sum. It is logical and right that the party least able afford to absorb the loss—the victim—be paid first. Several states and the federal government have already legislated such a priority.

Restitution Recommendation from the field #8

Corrections agencies, including prisons, jails, probation departments, and paroling authorities, should designate one person to be responsible for victim inquiries and contact regarding restitution. Victims are often confused about which official to call with questions and concerns about restitution because so many agencies are involved in the process. Designating one person or office for victims to contact for reliable and accurate information will help facilitate an effective restitution process.

Restitution Recommendation from the field #9

A probation or parole officer's proficiency in managing restitution cases should be a component of evaluating their job performance. The ability to manage restitution cases should be considered an essential part of a probation and parole officers' job. Evaluations of job performance should include this important responsibility.

Restitution Recommendation from the field #10

Failure to comply with a restitution order should result in an extended sentence of the offender's community supervision. In the state of Washington, offenders who fail to comply with their restitution orders can have their sentence of community supervision extended for up to 10 years by the department of corrections. Often, an offender's desire to be released from community supervision provides impetus for offenders to fulfill their restitution requirements in a more timely manner.

Restitution Recommendation from the field #11

Civil remedies should be applied on a routine and consistent basis to assist crime victims in collecting restitution. More than 40 states have enacted laws to provide civil remedies for the collection of court-ordered restitution. Such remedies include converting the restitution order into an automatic civil lien, garnishing wages, suspending driver's licenses, placing automatic liens on real property, and intercepting state income tax refunds. Agencies responsible for the collection of restitution should inform victims about these civil options. For a more detailed discussion of civil remedies, see the next chapter of this section.

Restitution Recommendation from the field #12

Victims should have the right to petition to amend the payment schedule for restitution, the amount of restitution ordered, and any failure to order restitution. Victims of crime frequently incur losses that are not known at the time of sentencing. Expenses for rehabilitation and long-term counseling as well as additional lost wages are often incurred following the sentence. Victims should have the right to petition the court to modify the restitution order. Several states have adopted this approach as a matter of law.

Restitution Recommendation from the field #13

Before the court modifies a payment plan or makes other changes to a restitution order, it should notify the victim and give them an opportunity to be heard on the matter. Of all the parties concerned, restitution orders affect the victim most. Any change in a restitution order must involve consideration of the victim's interests by soliciting input from the victim. Several states already provide victims this opportunity to be heard, and it should be standard practice in all states. In Arizona, the victim is also entitled to question the defendant under oath about his employment, assets, and financial condition."

I would just add here that we do need a restitution coordinator in every state corrections department and paroling authority and in every major probation department. Without one central coordinator these recommendations will have trouble getting implemented. Based on 39 years of experience with offenders I think one can use a carrot and a stick approach successfully to increase restitution payments to victims.. You can use gradually increased negative sanctions if an offender can pay restitution but fails to do so and you can increase positive sanctions for payments like early termination of supervision.

As a chaplain who has counseled hundreds of crime victims I think the way we do restitution in this country can be greatly improved which will lead to crime victims satisfaction about the handling of their criminal case. By receiving restitution the crime victim often has a feeling of fair and equitable treatment. By not receiving it at all or receiving significantly less than promised the ones financially harmed by the crime feel re-victimized or betrayed. When a victim receives no information about asking for restitution or there is no emphasis placed on it at sentencing through the victim impact statement then the losses will not be established that can be recovered through restitution. This leads to secondary victimization or a sense by the victim that the system failed him by failing to make him as financially whole as possible. This can be corrected with focused effort by the criminal justice system in my view and following many of the recommendations above.

Last but not least,

The actual words CRIMINAL JUSTICE SYSTEM need to be changed on every state and federal building to VICTIMS JUSTICE SYSTEM. That would, at the very least, begin a change in society's thinking—and lead to a change in our hearts and minds. We could take crime victims to the Inn of healing and give them whatever they need to get better. It is time!

References

Beloof, Douglas E., Paul G. Cassell and Steven J. Twist. *Victims in Criminal Procedure: Second Edition.* Durham: Carolina Academic Press, 2006.

Casarjian, Robin. *Forgiveness: A Bold Choice for a Peaceful Heart.* New York: Bantam, 1992.

Cheston, Sharon E. and Robert J. Wicks. *Essentials for Chaplains.* Mahwah, NJ: Paulist Press, 1993.

Clinebell, Howard. *Basic Types of Pastoral Care and Counseling: Resources for the Ministry of Healing and Growth.* New Haven: Yale University, 1984.

Collins, Gary R. *Christian Counseling: A Comprehensive Guide.* Third Edition. Nashville: Thomas Nelson, 2007.

Delaplane, David and Ann. *Victims: A Manual for Clergy and Congregations.* Denver: Spiritual Dimensions in Victims Services, 1997.

Figley, Charles. *Compassion Fatigue.* Elliott City: Chevron, 1994.

Herman, Judith Lewis. *Trauma and Recovery.* New York: Basicbooks of HarperCollins Publishers. 1992.

Hiltner, Seward. *Pastoral Counseling*. Nashville: Abingdon, 1949.

Hook, Melissa. *Ethics in Victim Services*. Baltimore: Sidran Institute Press, 2005.

Hunter, Rodney J., and Nancy J. Ramsey, eds. *Dictionary of Pastoral Care and Counseling*. Nashville: Abingdon, 2005.

Jones, L. Gregory. *Embodying Forgiveness: A Theological Analysis*. Grand Rapids: Willam B. Eerdmans Publishing Co., 1995.

JUSTPEACE. *Engaging Conflict Well*. Washington, D.C.: JUSTPEACE Center for Mediation and Conflict Transformation, 2006.

Lampman, Lisa Barnes, Editor. *God and the Victim*. Grand Rapids: William B. Eerdmans Publishing Co., 1999.

Lampman, Lisa, ed. *Helping a Neighbor in Crisis*. Wheaton, Ill.: Tyndale House Publishers, Inc., 1997.

Lord, Janice Harris, and Melissa Hook, Sharifa Alkhateeb, Sharon J. English. *Spiritually Sensitive Caregiving*: A Multi-Faith handbook. Burnsville: Compassion Press. 2008.

Magnani, Laura, and Harmon Wray. *Beyond Prison.*, Minneapolis: Fortress Press, 2006.

McCormack, Janet R., and Naomi K. Paget. *The Work of the Chaplain*. Valley Forge: Judson Press, 2006.

Mid-Atlantic Thresholds. *The Thresholds Volunteer Teacher's Manual*, Thornton, PA: Mid-Atlantic Thresholds, 2004.

Office for Victims of Crime, *New Directions from the Field: Victims Rights and Services for the 21st Century*, United States Department of Justice: Washington, D.C., 1998.

O 'Hara, Kathleen. *A Grief Like No Other*: Surviving the Violent Death of Someone You Love, New York: Marlowe and Co., 2006.

Patton, John. *Pastoral Care: An Essential Guide.* Nashville: Abingdon, 2005.

Peterson, Eugene H. The Message: The Bible in Contemporary Language. Colorado Springs:NavPress, 2002.

Peterson, Eugene H. *The Message: The Bible in Contemporary Language.* Colorado Springs:NavPress, 2002.

Spungeon, Deborah. *Homicide: The Hidden Victims A guide for Professionals.* Thousand Oaks: Sage Publications, 1998.

U.S. Department of Health and Human Services. *Mental Health Response to Mass Violence and Terrorism: A Training Manual.* DHHS Pub. No. SMA 3959. Rockville, MD: Center for Mental Health Services, Substance Abuse and Mental Health Services Administration, 2004.

Zehr, Howard. *Changing Lenses*, Scottdale: Herald Press, 1990.

Zehr, Howard. *The Little Book of Restorative Justice*, Intercourse: Good Books, 2002.

Appendix A:

Resources

A. Organizations

Anti-Violence Partnership of Philadelphia, 215-438-9070.
Association of Traumatic Stress Specialists, 512-868-3677.
Association for Death and Counseling, 860-586-7503.
Center for Loss and Life Transition, 970-226-6050.
Compassionate Friends, 708-990-0010.
Concerns of Police Survivors, 573-346-4911.
Crime Victims Advocacy Council, 770-333-9254.
Faith Trust Institute 877-860-2255.
International Critical Incident Stress Foundation, 420-730-4311.
International Society for Traumatic Stress Studies, 847-480-9028.
Maryland Crime Victims' Resource Center, Inc., 301-952-0063.
Mothers Against Drunk Driving, 800-Get-Madd.
National Center for Victims of Crime, 800-FYI-Call.
National Coalition of Homicide Survivors, 520-740-5729.
National Crime Prevention Council, 202-466-6272.
National Crime Victim Bar Association, 202-467-8753.
National Criminal Justice Reference Service, 800-851-3420.
National District Attorneys Association, 843-792-2942.

National Funeral Director's Association. 800-228-6322.
National Organization for Victims Assistance, 202-232-6682.
National Victims Constitutional Amendment Network, 303-832-1522.
Office for Victims of Crime, USDOJ, 202-307-5983.
Office for Victims of Crime Resource Center, 800-851-3420.
Parents of Murdered Children, 888-818-7662.
Sidran Institute, 410-825-8888.
Stand! Against Domestic Violence, 510-236-8972.
Tragedy Assistance Program for Survivors (TAPS), 800-959-8277.
Victim's Assistance Legal Organization, 703-748-0811.
Victims Assistance Online (Canadian) www.vaonline.org
Vidocq Society, 215-389-0299.

B. Chaplain Resources

American Association of Christian Counselors, 800-526-8673.
American Association of Marriage and Family Therapists, 703-838-9808.
American Association of Pastoral Counselors, 703-385-6967.
American Correctional Chaplains Association, 860-691-6549.
Association for Clinical Pastoral Education, 404-320-1472.
Association of Professional Chaplains, 847-240-1014.
College of Pastoral Supervision and Psychotherapy, 212-246-6410.
Council on Ministries in Specialized Settings, 757-728-3180.
International Conference of Police Chaplains, 850-654-9736.
National Association of Catholic Chaplains, 414-483-4898.
National Association of Jewish Chaplains, 973-929-3168.
National Center on Elder Abuse. 202-682-0100.
National Child Abuse Hotline, 800-4-A-Child.
National Conference on Ministry to the Armed Forces, 703-455-7908.
National Domestic Violence Hotline, 800-799-SAFE.
National Institute of Business and Industrial Chaplains, 713-266-2456.

Veterans Affairs Endorsing Chaplaincy, 703-455-7908.
Violence Against Women's Office, 202-307-6026.

C. Selected Endorsing Websites or Contacts for Chaplains

Alliance of Baptists, www.allianceofbaptists.org; American Baptist, www.abc-cpcs.org, Apostolic Catholic, www.apostoliccatholic.org, Assemblies of God, www.chaplaincy.ag.org, Disciples of Christ, kjones@dhm.disciples.org, Church of Christ, Garcia@church-of-Christ.org, Church of Jesus Christ of Latter-Day Saints, clawsonfw@ldschurch.org, Church of the Nazarene, djennings@nazarene.org, Conservative Baptist, www.cbcchaplains.net, Cooperative Baptist Fellowship, www.cbfnet.org, Episcopal, www.ecusa-chaplain.org, Lutheran, www.elca.org/chaplains, Islamic, www.siss.edu, Catholic Chaplains, www.nacc.org, National Baptist Convention of America, PastorD1953@yahoo.com, National Baptist Convention USA, gradyscott@aol.com, Jewish chaplains, www.jcca.org, Pentecostal Church of God, lmboyles@aol.com, Presbyterian, www.erols.com/pccmp and www.pcusa.org, Presbyterian Reformed, www.pcanet.org, Progressive National Baptist Convention, www.pnbc.org, Reformed Church in America, www.rca.org, Roman Catholic Church, consult Archdiocese/diocese, Seventh Day Adventists, www.adventistchaplains.org, Southern Baptist Convention North American Mission Board, www.namb.net/chaplain, United Church of Christ, www.ucc.org, United Methodist Church General Board of Higher Education and Ministry UMEA, www.gbhem.org/chaplains, United Pentecostal Church International, www.upci.org.

Appendix B:

Restorative Justice: An Annotated Bibliography

Useful Websites:

From http://new.gbgm-umc.org /missionstudies/restorativejustice/ bibliography/?search=restorative justice

Global Ministries website above published these resources below for a 2002-2003 mission study.

Restorative Justice: Moving Beyond Punishment by Harmon Wray with Leader's Guide by Brenda Connelly.

The past 20 years have seen a tremendous increase in the population of U.S. prisons. We have seen children who have committed crimes sentences to prison terms that will end long into their adulthood. Some prisons are run by corporations under government contract. Racial profiling, the death penalty, the rights of victims are all issues that impact and often divide Americans and United Methodists. *The Book of Resolutions of the United Methodist Church* devotes many pages to these issues and demands a response by the church. Harmon Wray writes a book that demands our attention and response. *The Leader's Guide* by Brenda Connelly offers a varied program of group activities designed for four two-hour sessions. Worship and Bible study are included in all sessions.

Youth Video with Guide

Justice 4 All

What happens when young people come into contact with the criminal justice system in the United States? This 20-minute video, broken into segments to use with a youth group or church school class, presents issues of justice and programs of restorative justice for young people. Includes a booklet of suggestions for presentation, discussion and action with resource list. Also informative for adult audiences - especially those interested in issues facing youth today.

Theology and Foundations

A. Companion, *Peace and Justice Shall Embrace: Toward Restorative Justice, a Prisoner's Perspective.* Iuniverse.com, 2001.

Practical, Biblical and human critique of the U.S. criminal justice systems from a priest-prisoner's perspective, with proposals and models for restorative justice reforms. Topics include: the relationship of poverty, race, mental illness and drug addiction to incarceration; capital punishment; the consequences of three-strikes and minimum-mandatory sentencing; the effects of politics on policy; inadequate legal representation for the poor.

Bazemore, S. Gordon, et al, eds. *Restorative Community Justice: Repairing Harm and Transforming Communities.* Anderson Pub Co, 2001.

Explores the foundations, stakeholders and organizational roles involved in restorative justice.

Braithwaite, John. *Restorative Justice and Responsive Regulation (Studies in Crime and Public Policy)* 2001.

Breton, Denise and Stephen Lehman. *The Mystic Heart of Justice: Restoring Wholeness in a Broken World.* Swedenborg Foundation, 2001.

Critique of the existing justice system, examining the pervasive feelings of guilt and failure, the sense of separateness that all external reward-and-punishment systems create.

Burton-Rose, Daniel, et al, eds. *The Celling of America: An Inside Look at the U.S. Prison Industry.* Common Courage Press, 1998.

Written by persons in prison about the conditions there.

Christie, Nils. *Crime Control as Industry: Towards Gulags, Western Style*. Routledge, 1993.

Argues that crime control, rather than crime itself, is the real danger for our future.

Close Encounters of the Justice System Kind: Theme Action Course for Older Youth. Sharon K. Youngs and Beth Basham. Presbyterian Distribution Service, 800-524-2612, 1997.

Covert, Henry G. *Ministry to the Incarcerated*. Loyola Press, 1995.

Explains how the inmate stresses of low self-esteem, guilt, unrealistic expectations can be major obstacles to rehabilitation and spiritual healing.

Cragg, Wesley. *The Practice of Punishment: Towards a Theory of Restorative Justice (Readings in Applied Ethics)* Routledge 1992).

Offers a comprehensive study of punishment that identifies the principles of sentencing and corrections on which modern correctional systems should be built.

Dear, John. *Peace Behind Bars: A Peacemaking Priest's Journal from Jail*. Theological Book Service, 1995.

Helps us to glimpse the world of prisoners and the soul of a committed Christian peacemaker.

Donziger, Steven R. *The Real War on Crime: The Report of the National Criminal Justice Commission*. Harper Perennial, 1996.

Examines a wide range of issues, including prison populations, crime rates, law enforcement, racial bias in the criminal justice system, and alternatives to incarceration.

Hadjor, Kofi Buenor. *Another America, The Politics of Race and Blame*, South End Press, 1995.

Hadley, Michael L. *The Spiritual Roots of Restorative Justice*. State University of NY, 2001.

Explores the concept of restorative justice in diverse spiritual traditions

Justice or "Just Deserts"? an Adult Study of the Restorative Justice Approach, Virginia Mackey and Carolyn Shadle. Presbyterian Criminal Justice Program, free, 888-728-7228.

Millard,Ted Grimsrud, Loren L. Johns, eds. *Peace and Justice Shall Embrace: Power and Theopolitics in the Bible: Essays in Honor of Millard Lind*. Pandora Pr USA, 2000.

Provides fresh exegetical insights from the Bible and penetrating theological analysis with regard to peace, justice, power, theopolitics. These essays shed new light on the politics of God and the peaceable character of biblical visions of justice.

Parenti, Christian. *Lockdown America: Police, and Prisons in the Age of Crisis*. Verso, 2000. Service Center Stock #3440,

Over 1.7 million Americans live in prisons, a 300% increase since 1980. In documenting the horrors corporate prisons, gang sweeps, border raids, and jailhouse violence, the author moves toward a deeper understanding of the links between crime and politics in a period of gathering economic crisis.

Reiman, Jeffrey H. *The Rich Get Richer and the Poor Get Prison: Ideology, Class, and Criminal Justice*, Allyn & Bacon, 1997.

Documents the extent of anti-poor bias in arrest, conviction, and sentencing practices and shows that the bias is conjoined with a general refusal to remedy the causes of crime - poverty, poor education, and discrimination. As a result, the criminal justice system fails to reduce crime.

Snyder, T. Richard. The *Protestant Ethic and the Spirit of Punishment*. Wm. B. Eerdmans, 2000.

Confronts the spirit of punishment that permeates our culture and its deleterious effects on today's penal system and society at large. Rooted in experiences of prison reality, the book sets forth an original theory about the theological roots of our current punitive ethos.

Strang, Heather, and John Braithwaite, eds. *Restorative Justice and Civil Society*. Cambridge U, 2001.

Van Ness, Daniel W. Karen Heetderks Strong. *Restoring Justice*. Anderson Pub Co 1997).

Overview of restorative justice: Its theory, principles and practices all under the umbrella of God's love and compassion for humanity. Resources for follow-up.

Wilkinson, Henrietta. *Victims of Crime: A Christian Perspective*. Presbyterian Distribution Service 800-524-2612, #258-90-707.

Alternative Models

Braswell, Michael, et al. *Corrections, Peacemaking, and Restorative Justice: Transforming Individuals and Institutions* Anderson Pub Co, 2000.

Breton, Denise and Stephen Lehman. *The Mystic Heart of Justice: Restoring Wholeness in a Broken World* 2001. $24.95

An alternative justice system that is not from "outside in" but "inside out.": Looking at examples among Native Americans, the authors show that many human cultures over thousands of years flourished without resorting to reward-punishment systems. Indigenous peoples, for instance, affirmed the uniqueness of each individual, crafting social forms that drew out that uniqueness. The results were cohesive societies that can serve as models for changing our fundamental approach to fairness today.

Coleman, John W. Jr. *Breaking Walls Building Bridges: Confronting Violence in the United States through Mission Outreach*, General Board of Global Ministries, United Methodist Church, 1997.

Tells the stories of community and institutional projects and programs. (For more information, click here.)

Furio, Jennifer. *Restorative Justice*. Algora Pub 2002.

Galaway, Burt and Joe Hudson, eds. *Restorative Justice: International Perspectives*. Criminal Justice Press and Kugler Publications, 1996.

Gerry, Johnstone. *Restorative Justice: Ideas, Practices, Debates* Willan Pub, 2002.

Mackey, Virginia. *Restorative Justice: Toward Nonviolence*, Presbyterian Distribution Service, 800-524-2612.

McGarrel, Ed, et al. *Returning Justice to the Community: The Indianapolis Juvenile Restorative Justice Experiment*. Hudson Institute 2000.

In the early 1990s the Kansas City Police Department experimented with a proactive philosophy of crime reduction called directed police patrolling. The initiative swam against the current of contemporary criminology, which maintains that crime is largely the mere result of poverty, racial injustice.

Miller, Melissa A. *Family Violence, The Compassionate Church Responds*. Herald, 1994.

Morris, Allison, Gabrielle Maxwell eds. *Restorative Justice for Juveniles: Conferencing, Mediation and Circles.*International Specialized Book Service, 2001.

Office of Juvenile Justice and Delinquency Prevention. Guide for Implementing the Balanced and Restorative Model online document at http:// www.ojjdp.ncjrs.org/pubs/implementing/contents/html.

Rigby, Andrew. *Justice and Reconciliation: After the Violence.* Lynne Rienner Publishers, 2001.

Scheck, Barry, Peter Neufeld and Jim Dwyer. *Actual Innocence: When Justice Goes Wrong and How to Make It Right.* Penguin Putnam, 2001.

This book offers a look into the inadequacies of a criminal justice system in disarray through the stories of ten innocent people who were finally freed due to the work of dedicated crusaders.

Sharpe, Susan. *Restorative Justice: A Vision for Healing and Change.* Edmonton Victim Offender Mediation Society, 1998.

Strang, Heather,et al, eds. *Restorative Justice.* Ashgate Publishing Company, 2000.

Sullivan, Dennis and Larry Tifft. *Restorative Justice: Healing the Foundations of Our Everyday Lives,* Criminal Justice Pr, 2001.

Poses a radical critique of current criminal justice practices in favor of a restorative justice alternative. Then, it advocates a fundamental reformulation of the thinking and practices of restorative justice itself. The authors call for two sweeping revisions in restorative justice thinking: (1)replacing justice practices based on rights and "deserts" with approaches that seek to meet the needs of all — including the harm-doer and the community, as well as those directly affected by a harm; and (2) applying these principles beyond the justice system to a broad range of social institutions, including families, schools, workplaces and neighborhoods. The book offers many concrete examples of the type of need-based restorative justice that is being proposed

Van Wormer, Katherine S. *Counseling Female Offenders and Victims: A Strengths Restorative Approach.* Springer Series of Family Violence. Springer Pub Co, 2001.

Walgrave, Lode, Gordon Bazemore eds. *Restorative Juvenile Justice: Repairing the Harm of Youth Crime.* Willow Tree Pr, 1999.

Zehr, Howard J. *Changing Lenses: A New Focus for Crime and Justice.* Herald Press, 1990.

Examines the paradigm of retributive justice and proposes restorative justice.

In National and Global Scenes

Barkan, Elazar, *The Guilt of Nations: Restitution and Negotiating Historical Injustices.* Johns Hopkins, 2001.

How should nations deal with gross inhumanity? Since World War II, individual nations and international groups have been struggling with that issue. Examines a wide range of historical injustices within and between nations over the past 50 years, urging that we move toward a theory of restitution that allows victims and perpetrators to negotiate their understandings of history and identity and to establish a basis for a common future. Most of Barkan's book is devoted to analysis of specifics: the Holocaust; U.S. internment of Japanese Americans; Nazi art in Russian museums and Nazi gold in Swiss banks; Japanese abuse of "comfort women"; Eastern Europe after decades of Communism; treatment of indigenous groups on the U.S. mainland, in Hawaii, in Australia, and in New Zealand; and the issue of restitution for slavery in the U.S. His final chapter draws lessons from these case studies, working "Toward a Theory of Restitution."

Biggar, Nigel, ed. *Burying the Past: Making Peace and Doing Justice After Civil Conflict*. Georgetown University Press, 2001.

Focusing the problems of establishing democracy after a transition from brutal, oppressive regimes — and often-violent civil, prolonged conflict. The problem is to reconcile the populace so that reprisals and revenge do not undermine or subvert the newly establishing democratic principles, procedures, and compromises.

Boraine, Alex, *A Country Unmasked: Inside South Africa's Truth and Reconciliation Commission,* London: Oxford University Press, 2000.

Botman, M. Russell and Peterson, Robin M., editors, *To Remember and to Heal: Theological & Psychological Reflections on Truth and Reconciliation.*

Galaway, Burt and Hudson, Joe, editors, *Restorative Justice: International Perspectives*, Monsey: Criminal Justice Press, 1996.

Hayner, Priscilla B., *Unspeakable Truths: Confronting State Terror and Atrocity*, Routledge, 2000.

Jeffrey, Paul, *Recovering Memory: Guatemalan Churches and the Challenge of Peacemaking*, Uppsala: Life and Peace Institute, 1998.

Krog, Antjie, *Country of My Skull: Guilt, Sorrow & The Limits of Forgiveness in the New South Africa*, New York: Three Rivers Press, 1998.

Maguire Marread Corriger, *The Vision of Peace: Faith and Hope in Northern Ireland*, Maryknoll: Orbis, 1999.

McCartney, Clem, editor, *Accord: Striking a Balance; The Northern Ireland Peace Process* London: Conciliation Resources, 1999.

Mulunda-Nyanga, Ngoy Daniel, *The Reconstruction of Africa: Faith and Freedom for a Conflicted Continent*, Nairobi: All Africa Conference of Churches, 1997.

Rigby, Andrew. *Justice and Reconciliation: After the Violence.* Lynne Rienner, 2001.

Ross, Rupert, *Return to the Teachings: Exploring Aboriginal Justice*, Toronto: Penguin, 1996.

Tutu, Desmond, *No Future Without Forgiveness*, New York: Doubleday, 1999.

Draws upon the experiences of persons in South America, South Africa and Europe.

Appendix C:

Message on New Directions

"U.S. Department of Justice
Office of Justice Programs
Office for Victims of Crime

New Directions from the Field: Victims' Rights and Services for the 21st Century is a comprehensive report and set of recommendations on victims' rights and services from and concerning virtually every community involved with crime victims across the nation. The report represents a significant maturation in the field of victims' rights and services since the President's Task Force on Victims of Crime released its Final Report in 1982. New Directions chronicles the extraordinary accomplishments of a still young field, but also recommends what we as a society should strive to achieve for victims as we enter the 21st century.

New Directions is the culmination of more than 3 years' work by over 1,000 individuals in the victims field including crime victims, representatives from national victim advocacy and service organizations, criminal justice practitioners, allied professionals, and many others. In addition, literally hundreds of reference documents were utilized and listed in the endnotes of each of the 18 chapters. The work of these individuals and the publication and dissemination of this material has been supported by the Office for Victims of Crime (OVC). The report and recommendations represent views from the field, however, and do not necessarily reflect the views of the Department of Justice. Moreover, while the recommendations may not reflect all of the individual contributors' views, the contributors agree that all of the recommendations are worthy of discussion and consideration.

This bulletin is a reprint of chapter 11 from New Directions and deals specifically with promising practices and recommendations related to the Faith Community. As we move into the 21st century, New Directions should serve as a vitally useful guide for developing policies, programs, and practices on behalf of crime victims well into the next century. As comprehensive as this report is, however, the real challenge begins now. After you read the recommendations, after you have examined the numerous promising practices presented in each section, then I encourage you to move forward to see how you can implement improvements in a manner that meets the needs of crime victims.

Kathryn M. Turman
Acting Director
Office for Victims of Crime"

Appendix D:

New Directions from the Field

Victims' Rights and Services for the 21st Century
Faith Community

Our families are torn by violence. Our communities are destroyed by violence. Our faith is tested by violence. We have an obligation to respond. (Pastoral Message, U.S. Catholic Conference, 1994)

Tens of millions of Americans call upon clergy and religious leaders for spiritual guidance, support, and information in times of personal crisis. One study found that people in crisis due to the death of someone close were almost five times more likely to seek the aid of a clergy person than all other mental health sources combined. While the faith community has historically provided prison ministry programs, few religious institutions have developed programs specifically to serve victims of crime.

Faith-based crime victim assistance programs were virtually nonexistent in 1982 when the President's Task Force on Victims of Crime released its Final Report. The Task Force encouraged the faith community to recognize that "the victim certainly no less than the victimizer is in need of aid, comfort, and spiritual ministry." It recommended that the ministry develop both seminary and inservice training on the criminal justice system, the needs of victims, and ways to restore victims' spiritual and material health.

The faith community has made steady progress toward these goals. With support from the Office for Victims of Crime (OVC), educational initiatives on victim assistance have been developed in communities across the country. Led by groups such as The Spiritual Dimension in Victim Services in Denver, Colorado, these initiatives have included training for parish clergy and hospital chaplains conducting ministries in high-crime urban areas, training for crime victim service providers seeking ways to involve the faith community in their efforts, workshops at national and regional denominational events, and distribution of manuals, brochures, and other materials on victim assistance to clergy and congregations.

This section describes the wide range of victim assistance programs established by the faith community in the past 15 years and suggests specific ways in which communities of faith can more effectively assist victims of crime.

Faith-Based Victim Assistance Programs

In communities across the country, faith-based victim assistance programs have grown in number and expanded the services that they provide. They are now an important source of support to victims and their families.

In Akron, Ohio, the Furnace Street Mission established one of the first faith-based victim assistance programs in the United States in 1982. Today it serves more than 25,000 people a year, exemplifying how traditional ministries can be expanded to include crime victim assistance.

Neighbors Who Care, an interdenominational program, was founded in 1992 as the victim-serving subsidiary of the large national organization, Prison Fellowship. The program enlists volunteers from churches to provide direct services, primarily to victims of property crime. Volunteers repair property and provide transportation, moving assistance, and other vital services. The program recently expanded to include services to victims of domestic violence and other crimes.

African-American churches in the East Bay communities of Northern California have joined together to conduct neighborhood meetings and counseling after violent crimes and instances of police officer misconduct.

In Jackson, Mississippi, Catholic Charities sponsors a shelter for battered families that serves 350 women and children each year from seven rural counties, providing transitional housing, legal assistance, and individual and group counseling.

The United States Catholic Conference has developed a number of publications on crime victims' issues. Confronting a Culture of Violence A Catholic Framework for Action highlights a number of victim assistance and crime prevention activities in dioceses, parishes, and schools across the country and calls for a major effort to mobilize the Catholic community to confront the culture of violence. When I Call for Help A Pastoral Response to Domestic Violence Against Women contains practical suggestions for assisting women who are battered as well as men who abuse. Walk in the Light A Pastoral Response to Child Sexual Abuse reaches out to people who have been abused, to abusers, and to pastors, pastoral staff, and other church workers who can assist victims.

Brother Modesto Leon of the Catholic Church in Los Angeles operates a support and intervention program for mothers of murdered Latino children. The mothers comfort each other and tell their stories to gang members to prevent further gang violence and death in the Los Angeles Latino community.

In Memphis, Tennessee, Victims to Victory provides faith centered support and healing to homicide survivors. Katherine (Kitty) Lawson, an African-American ordained minister at Abundant Grace Fellowship Church, founded Victims to Victory in 1995 in response to the needs of a church family tormented by a double murder.

Religious and spiritual organizations frequently invite victim assistance organizations to use their space to conduct support groups, candlelight vigils, and other victim assistance activities. In Cleveland, Mississippi, for example, Pastor Roderick Mitchell opened his church in 1995 to a rape crisis program in need of a home. The church has now expanded to provide services to all victims of crime through a community-based organization called Exodus Center for Life.

The Christian Society for the Healing of Dissociative Disorders is a national consortium of psychiatrists, psychologists, and social workers who combine therapeutic skill and spirituality in treating ritualistically abused survivors. The Society is headquartered in Bedford, Texas, and holds an annual conference of several hundred participants to share treatment information.

Multidisciplinary Efforts

One of the most promising areas of the faith community's response to the victims' movement has been the willingness of religious organizations to collaborate with the secular victim assistance community. The programs discussed below illustrate how communities of faith can work with organizations pursuing similar goals to provide comprehensive services to crime victims.

Faith communities are "adopting" child protection social workers, serving as a resource for them as they help children recover from family violence. The programs, which have a significant presence in California, Oklahoma, and other states, also help to educate congregations about child abuse and neglect and the large numbers of children who suffer from these crimes.

In Costa Mesa, California, Royal Family Kids Camps help congregations sponsor summer camps for severely abused and neglected children. To date, more than 4,000 children between the ages of 7 and 11 who are in the custody of child protective services have enjoyed a week of positive support in a safe and nurturing environment.

The Center for Prevention of Sexual and Domestic Violence, affiliated with the United Church of Christ of Seattle, Washington, directly supports victims and survivors and promotes cooperation between communities of faith and secular organizations across the country on sexual and domestic violence issues. The center recently expanded its activities to include education on clergy sexual misconduct and assistance to the victims of this crime.

The Colorado/Oklahoma Resource Council (CORC), a secular organization, was formed in Denver, Colorado, to provide resources to victims of the bombing of the Alfred P. Murrah Federal Building in Oklahoma City after the trial was moved to Denver, Colorado. CORC established a spiritual needs committee to support those attending the trial. CORC, the Denver Police Chaplaincy Corps, the Colorado Council of Churches, The Spiritual Dimension in Victim Services, and other organizations have established a multifaith coalition to assist and provide counseling to the families.

Victim-Offender Dialogue

The community of faith has created numerous faith-based victim-offender mediation/dialogue programs in which meetings between victims and offenders are arranged when victims request it and the courts allow offenders to participate. Mediation/dialogue programs allow offenders to confront the consequences of their crimes and then work out contracts with victims to provide them with restitution. Volunteers from the faith community are trained by professional mediators to facilitate the dialogue, which must be undertaken with great care to ensure that victims and offenders are prepared adequately for what can be a painful healing process.

The Mennonite-based Victim Offender Reconciliation Program in Clovis, California, offers victim-offender dialogue services that have been used widely in other communities of faith to help individuals start the recovery process in the aftermath of victimization. The program is supported by 42 churches and provides training to Christian and Jewish communities.

Confidentiality and Reporting Crime to Law Enforcement

Religious leaders are responsible for ministering to all members of their congregations, including those who may have committed criminal acts. This obligation presents ethical and religious dilemmas when crimes are confessed in confidentiality, especially if the criminal activity is continuing. In these situations, clergy must weigh the importance of respecting privileged communication in relation to the need to protect victims and society from harm. To make responsible decisions, clergy must have a full understanding of the law as well as the nature and consequences of victimization.

Laws requiring the reporting of suspected child abuse highlight this dilemma. All states mandate the reporting of child abuse by professionals who come into contact with children, and at least 30 states require clergy to report child abuse in some circumstances. Only five of these states, however, clearly require clergy to report in all circumstances, leaving largely intact the traditional privilege given to communication with clergy. But an increasing number of faith communities are modifying their codes of clergy conduct to require clergy to report suspected child abuse and complete training on child abuse issues.

The Evangelical Lutheran Church in America gives this directive to clergy: "Ordained ministers must respect privileged and confidential communication and may not disclose such communication, except with the express permission of the person who has confided it or if the person is perceived to intend great harm to self or others."

The Episcopalian Church requires 4 hours of training on child abuse for those who work with children during their daily activities. This requirement applies to all religious leaders as well as day care providers. In addition, the Roman Catholic Church requires some Archdiocese to receive similar training.

Recommendations from the Field for the Faith Community

Faith Community Recommendation from the Field #1

The faith community should recognize that the victim, no less than the victimizer, is in need of aid, comfort, and spiritual ministry, and faith-based congregations and organizations should provide assistance to victims whenever possible.

There continues to be a general lack of education and understanding of the needs of crime victims in the faith community. Recognition of crime victims' needs should be an integral part of the faith community's worship, life, and ministry.

In a 1992 survey of 97 denominational headquarters, respondents were asked about their programs to assist crime victims. Most replied that their programs were jail and prison ministries for offenders, not victims. While these programs should not be diminished, it is insufficient for the faith community to address the spiritual needs of offenders without recognizing the spiritual needs of victims. The faith community can and should conduct ministries for both.

While many denominations have mission statements that address child abuse and neglect and domestic violence, these mission statements should be expanded to include all victims of crime. All denominations should adopt such statements and include them in canons of ethics.

Many excellent examples of programs have been created and supported by the faith community, from providing emergency property repair, transportation, and other crisis services to supporting summer camps for child abuse victims. These efforts should be expanded.

Faith Community Recommendation from the Field #2

Courses on crime victimization and crime victim assistance should be established in clergy educational institutions and theological seminaries, including both worship and pastoral counseling courses.

Because so many people in crisis seek clergy for assistance, professional schools that educate future religious and spiritual leaders must provide a foundation of knowledge in the field of victim issues. Classes should include the clergy's role in intervening with crime victims, appropriate courses of action that involve criminal justice, medical, mental health, and social services referrals, and planning of worship services centered around a crisis. Clergy should have education in appropriate death notification following a sudden death as compared to death following illness.

Faith Community Recommendation from the Field #3

Continuing education on crime victimization and crime victim assistance should be provided for all clergy and religious leaders, including chaplains in hospitals, police departments, and the military and other individuals within the faith community who may come into contact with victims.

Education about the consequences of victimization will increase the faith community's responsiveness to crime victims. To help spiritual and religious leaders appropriately treat or refer serious trauma-related cases that require indepth mental health intervention, they should be trained to recognize symptoms of post-traumatic stress disorder and other long-term psychological reactions to crime victimization. They should also be knowledgeable about community, state, and national resources that provide victim assistance.

Religious leaders often are among the first responders following a sudden, violent death. Although most clergy are educated in traditional grief counseling techniques, education on specific interventions for trauma, grief, and loss following criminal victimization should be provided. Clergy should also receive training on appropriate death notification practices.

Other groups within the faith community also interact with victims and need education about victims' issues and services. They include Sunday school teachers, youth leaders, choir directors, and counselors on prayer phone lines providing comfort and assistance to individuals in crisis. Religious and spiritual organizations should identify such groups within their memberships and make continuing education on victims' issues and services available to them.

Faith Community Recommendation from the Field #4

Religious institutions at all levels should cooperate with victim assistance agencies and organizations to offer joint services to victims of crime and to disseminate publications on crime victim assistance.

Religious organizations working in conjunction with victim assistance agencies have the capacity to provide important services to crime victims. During the trials of the bombing of the Alfred P. Murrah Federal Building, for example, safe havens were established in local churches by victim assistance providers to ensure that victims would have a quiet place to meet and receive counseling. In another collaborative effort, the National Cathedral in Washington, D.C., worked with Mothers Against Drunk Driving to hold the International Candlelight Vigil of Remembrance and Hope in December 1997, which featured the voices of victims and survivors of crime.

Efforts must be expanded to distribute victim assistance information, including booklets, pamphlets, videos, and educational materials, more widely in the community of faith. Ministerial associations and interfaith alliances should be included routinely in the dissemination of victim service information.

Faith Community Recommendation from the Field #5

The clergy should provide training for victim assistance providers, criminal justice officials, state victim assistance administrators, compensation program directors, and other public officials about the important role they can play in assisting victims.

State administrators, criminal justice-based victim assistance providers, and other public officials are often uncomfortable dealing with the faith community because they fear a blurring of the separation of church and state. The victim assistance community should recognize that faith-based programs can play a significant role in victim support as long as public funds are not used to promote specific sectarian beliefs. Victim service providers should ask clergy to help them react appropriately to people whose victimization includes a faith crisis.

Faith Community Recommendation from the Field #6

Requiring clergy to report suspected cases of child abuse should be seriously considered by religious institutions and governmental agencies, and appropriate policies should be developed to ensure the protection of children. Even in cases involving confidential communications, the clergy should hold the needs of children paramount and recognize their moral responsibility to help and protect child victims.

Recently, many state legislatures have considered whether clergy should be among those mandated to report child abuse and neglect in view of their legal privilege of confidentiality. The results have been mixed, with some states requiring clergy to report in all cases, other states requiring reporting in selected cases, and most states exempting clergy from reporting requirements when an offense is revealed in a confidential pastoral counseling or confessional setting. However, all states require clergy to report incidents of suspected child abuse while serving as therapists, school administrators, or day care providers.

Faith Community Recommendation from the Field #7

Communities of faith should hold clergy and other religious leaders in positions of trust within their congregations accountable for crimes they commit, including sexual acts against adults and children. Policies and procedures should be developed to ensure that appropriate cases of clergy misconduct are referred to law enforcement agencies.

Criminal background checks should be mandatory for all clergy, faith community staff, and volunteers who work with children. A number of high-profile civil legal actions have been brought against religious leaders accused of child abuse or sexual assault and their religious institutions for not reporting known incidents of abuse to law enforcement agencies. While those who commit such acts represent a small percentage of the faith community, it is crucial that policies and procedures be developed to ensure that these cases are handled with utmost concern for the victim and that appropriate cases are not only referred to law enforcement agencies but dealt with swiftly within the institution to ensure the protection of others.

Faith Community Recommendation from the Field #8

Religious and spiritual leaders should be encouraged to use their pulpits to educate and sensitize their congregations about crime and victimization issues.

Religious and spiritual leaders have an opportunity to use their positions to educate their congregations about crime and its impact information that could help the members of a congregation seek out the services they need if they become victims of crime. Religious and spiritual leaders could encourage congregations to join in the national October observance of "Domestic Violence Awareness Month" and deliver at least one sermon that month about the impact of family violence. In addition, they could highlight crime victims' issues during National Crime Victims' Rights Week, generally held at the end of April. Each year, the Office for Victims of Crime funds a National Crime Victims' Rights Week kit which includes a sample sermon about victims' issues.

Faith Community Recommendation from the Field #9

Religious and spiritual leaders should be willing to serve in leadership roles on community crisis response teams providing services in the aftermath of mass violence and other crimes that have significant impact upon entire communities.

Religious and spiritual leaders can play a leadership role in helping to ensure that their communities are prepared to respond to community and individual needs following incidents of mass violence, terrorism, or other major crimes. They can also volunteer to serve on crisis response teams that provide assistance to other communities, such as the teams organized by the National Organization for Victim Assistance to debrief school children, teachers, and emergency responders following the bombing of the Alfred P. Murrah Federal Building."

Appendix E:

Sample Victim Impact Statement

VICTIM IMPACT STATEMENT

Claudia Barnes

"Is it Friday yet?" These words were a weekly tradition for 13 years between Rowland and me. We always looked forward to our Friday night date. More times than not, we went to our favorite Mexican restaurant and met up with friends. That tragic morning, his words were: "I don't want to do this today. I want to stay in bed and snuggle some more." After getting ready for work, some of his last words to me were: "I have to go into the office early this morning, so we will have to ride separate. I've had a civil motion added to my calendar today, and I'm in the middle of a rape trial. I have to go over the jury charges." He then kissed me for the last time, telling me: "I'll see you in a little while, my love. Have I told you lately how much I love you?"

Hearing all of the sirens and commotion outside my office window, I looked out to see several Sheriff's deputies with their guns drawn on the sidewalk and noticed police cars blocking the intersections around the courthouse. Several of my co-workers gathered with me at the end of the hallway to see if we could see what was happening towards Underground Atlanta. News had reached me that one of the judges on the 8th floor of the old courthouse had been shot, but I had no idea that it was Rowland - would never have dreamed it could happen. I had no clue that anything was amiss in the courtroom for almost 40 minutes past the time he was shot. But, my knees buckled when my friend came and took me by the hand and told me to come with her. At that point, I knew the love of my life was the victim. "Maybe he's only wounded and will be ok", I kept saying. My heart was pounding, my body shaking as we ran over to my husband's chambers, passing his clerk in the hallway, who was in shock and had blood splatters on her arm. I had to grit my teeth to stay focused.

Gathered in front of the courtroom were so many deputies. My head was spinning, my heart pounding. I was whisked off to a jury room full of people staring at the floor and who were surrounded by paramedics. I began asking questions: "Who are you? Who are all these people?" No one would answer me, but I was persistent. One gentleman answered that he was a lawyer in the courtroom, and I replied, "But you are not with the DA's office." He said he was there because of a civil motion (then I remembered what Rowland had said about this before leaving home). Paramedics took my blood pressure, and I was moved again and again and again. A different, very good friend told me the devastating news. It was many hours before I was able to walk through my front door at home with the griping reminder that Rowland would not be coming home to be ever again.

That day has haunted me over and over - a bullet to the brain of such an intelligent, loving person. There is never a day that goes by that I do not re-enact what I think the scene to be, and it all seems like a nightmare that I can't erase from my thoughts; the murder and the end of the life of a great American who loved his fellow man and his judgeship because it afforded him the chance to make a difference in society. Rowland truly believed that the Courts (the judges) are the guardians of our freedom, and he gave his life in carrying out that duty. A staunch advocate of education, he always took the opportunity to speak to young people about taking advantage of higher learning. And he adored, and was always on call for, his friends and family. Rowland was a person who gave many people a break to begin their lives over again, and who was equally fair to all ages and races.

I lost my husband and soul mate, my best friend, the love of my life, my companion and lover, my daily source of entertainment, my retirement partner, a father, and also a step-father to my children. He will not come home from a week-long seminar, or after a mentally-taxing day at work, ready to let me pamper him. Other than in my mind, I will never again hear the voice that fascinated me, that said the sweet words, "Honey, oh love of my life, I'm home", or "Thank you for marrying me", or "Come sit next to me and let's watch the news." Other than in my mind, I will never again hear the voice that made me beam or break out in uncontrollable laughter. Nor will I wake up to the magic we possessed as a couple or experience the wonderful smell of his cologne. Instead, I will wake up to the startling thought that I hope the love of my life did not suffer. I have lost my good friend, Julie, who I also hope did not suffer, and have seen my other friends physically and emotionally damaged from this - another double whammy from the nature of the offense and the trauma of it all for me personally. It is a tragedy beyond words for such vibrant lives to have been cut short so cruelly.

On March 11, 2005, I became a member of a club that I did not want to join. I went to memorial services and to see my friend, Deputy Cynthia Hall. During the planning of a memorial service for Rowland, I asked for permission to go and hold hands with my loved one for the last time before he was cremated, because he and I held hands constantly for 13 years. Touching his hands, an important part of our relationship, linking my fingers with his, and running my fingers close to his temples where the bullet entered and exited, then down through the beard that I always kept trimmed, was an urgent and necessary act for me. I needed to see for myself that he was actually dead and that this was not a bad dream.

Getting to work the first day back on the job was excruciating. Nausea controlled my whole ride in. Today, my heart still skips a beat when I hear sirens or at times when I am walking the same halls at work that Rowland walked, with and without me by his side. There are days when stress gets the best of me, and the skin on my hands breaks out, sending me to the doctor. Some days I have no energy and have to force myself to go through the motions and thought processes of work and play. Now, going home each day to the void is sometimes overwhelming, and I feel helpless. Rowland is not here to ride to and from work with, to discuss events of the day, or to have a wonderful laugh together. Each birthday, anniversary, Father's Day, major holiday or family gathering is spent missing my special person and remembering past celebrations. My life consists of much decision making and realizing that I alone have to handle all matters and decisions of daily living. Because of this tragedy, I have suffered feelings of anxiety, the disruption of my life, an unbelievable sense of devastation, and have needed, and received, many types of support from former and newly-acquired friends - physical, emotional and spiritual to name a few. My faith in God has allowed me to remain sane as I strive to move forward and not stay in neutral, because my heart is truly broken.

Psychologically, I am still devastated by this horrible crime. Emotionally, I deal daily with sadness and anger and sometimes even fear. At times it seems almost too much for me, but I try to do the best that I can. No one should have to experience the level of horror that I have experienced. Our life together was not long enough.

The End and Amen from Chaplain Cook:

All the glory and honor goes to God for anything I ever did in His name. The people in all these stories deserved His love and I was honored to be His conduit.

CPSIA information can be obtained
at www.ICGtesting.com
Printed in the USA
BVHW031728170419
545819BV00001B/17/P